WILDLIFE TRAVELLER SCOTTISH ISLANDS

published by
pocket mountains ltd
6 Church Wynd, Bo'ness EH51 0AN
www.pocketmountains.com

ISBN: 0-9550822-4-2
EAN: 978-0-95508-224-5

Photography copyright © Richard Rowe. Additional photography copyright © Andy Hay/RSPB Images, page: 15; Iain Erskine, pages: 16/17; David Leaver/www.guideliner.co.uk, pages: 21, 33; Laurie Campbell, pages: 27, 67, 71; Peter Cairns/www.northshots.com, pages: 29, 89; Chris Rodger, page: 35; Colin Speedie/Shark Foundation, pages 37, 41; Ian French/Gairloch Marine Life Centre, page: 57; Peter Hizzett/Gemini Explorer, page: 59; Steve Knell/RSPB Images, page: 85; Dave Wheeler, page: 94

A catalogue record for this book is available from the British Library

Printed in Poland

Introduction

Scotland is renowned for its dramatic scenery, but the wildlife that inhabits it is rather less familiar. For a small country, Scotland contains a diverse mix of habitat that in turn supports an enviable array of plants and animals – often in prolific numbers.

This guide contains 40 wildlife destinations in Scotland's islands, journeying from the Inner Hebrides to the Western Isles (Outer Hebrides) and north to Orkney and Shetland.

Classic Scottish species such as red deer and golden eagle are present, but so too are vast numbers of wintering and breeding birds - including several million seabirds – and a high density of otters. Scotland also holds Europe's largest population of seals, while several of the 20 or so species of cetacean (whales, dolphins and porpoises) recorded in Scottish waters are relatively common.

Destinations in this guide have been chosen to reflect the variety of habitat found on each island and its relevance to particular wildlife. Some animals are easily seen, while others require more patience – and understanding.

Many of the destinations are reserves managed by charities and agencies such as the RSPB and Scottish Natural Heritage (SNH) and are easily enjoyed by all. Others involve more rugged expeditions, some with lengthy sea crossings

A car can serve as an ideal 'hide' when viewing wary species or those that are vulnerable to disturbance. But where possible and conditions allow, visitors are encouraged to embrace the spirit of adventure inherent in these islands by exploring on foot, by bike or from the water.

Visitors can minimise their impact on the environment, and maintain good relations with local inhabitants by keeping to purpose built paths where they exist, restricting the use of bikes to tracks, parking sensibly and avoiding fires and litter. Sadly, dogs and wildlife do not mix: check locally and use common sense. And always use a lead when around grazing land and during lambing.

How to use this guide

The destinations in this guide are divided into five regions, each covering an island grouping. The opening section for each region introduces the key features of the island group, together with a regional map. Brief access information and a relevant Ordnance Survey (OS) map for detailed navigation are provided at the beginning of individual location entries.

Many of the RSPB, SNH and other managed reserves have information centres and good trail maps onsite, while staff are often available to answer questions. In more remote locations, it is worth checking at ferry terminals, local shops and information points for details on guided walks and wildlife sightings.

Most west coast ferries are operated by Caledonian MacBrayne, although smaller operators serve several of the islands. Orkney and Shetland are both served by NorthLink Ferries, while Pentland Ferries and John O'Groats Ferries also operate to Orkney. The islands within Orkney and Shetland are linked by frequent inter-island services. Many islands can also be reached by air.

Responsible wildlife watching

The growing popularity of wildlife-based tourism has lengthened the traditional season in Scotland, bringing jobs and visitors to remote communities well into shoulder periods. It has also spawned a growth in land- and marine-based wildlife tour operators. Most are highly professional and follow strict codes of conduct. For your own enjoyment, and the sake of the wildlife you hope to see, these are the operators you should book with.

For guidance, members of Wild Scotland – an association of wildlife tourism operators – adhere to a charter that puts wildlife welfare first, while many marine operators have signed up to the Scottish Marine Wildlife Operators Association's voluntary code of conduct. SNH, the Scottish Executive's environment agency, is developing its own Marine Wildlife Watching Code to fulfil the requirements of the Nature Conservation (Scotland) Act 2004.

Wildlife watchers also have an important individual responsibility. Scotland's most vulnerable species are protected under the Wildlife and Countryside Act 1981. Amendments brought about by the Nature Conservation (Scotland) Act 2004 make it a criminal offence to intentionally or recklessly disturb any birds included in Schedule 1 of the Act whilst on or near the nest, while a licence is also required from SNH to photograph Schedule 1 species at the nest. Animals listed on Schedule 5 of the Act are afforded similar protection. For more information, visit the SNH website (www.snh.org.uk).

Sadly, egg collecting remains a problem and the nest sites of rare species are kept quiet out of necessity. Any suspicious activity should be reported to local police. All forces now have dedicated wildlife crime officers.

When to visit

Scotland has year-round wildlife appeal, although there are peaks in activity through the seasons. Here are some general periods to be aware of:

February to October gannets at colonies
April displaying waders, 'sky dancing' hen harriers
May corncrake arrive from Africa
May to mid-July majority of seabirds at colonies
May to September increased whale and dolphin activity, plus basking sharks
June common seals pup, red deer calve
June to July machair grassland in full bloom
Late-September to October red deer rut
September to March wintering geese and

swans from the north, large flocks of ducks and waders
October to November grey seals pup

Risks and how to avoid them

Some of the destinations in this guide require care, particularly around sea cliffs and when exploring more remote islands. When setting out on longer expeditions, consider your fitness, check regional weather forecasts and pack sensibly. Even in summer, it is recommended to take warm, waterproof clothing, although it is not advisable to wear waterproofs near cliff edges – a slip here could be fatal. For longer trips, take plenty of food and water and leave a route plan with a friend or relative in case of emergency. Seasickness tablets and midge repellent are also worth carrying.

Access

The Land Reform (Scotland) Act introduced in 2003 provided an official stamp on the 'right to roam', although in many respects it simply reinforced a strong tradition of public access to the countryside for recreational purposes. A key difference, however, is that under the Act the right of access depends on whether it is exercised responsibly.

Similarly, landowners also have an obligation not to

unreasonably prevent or deter those seeking access. The responsibilities of the public and land managers are now set out in the Scottish Outdoor Access Code.

However, at certain times of the year there are special restrictions that should be respected. These often concern farming, shooting and forest activities: if in any doubt, ask. Signs are usually posted at main access points with details. There should be no expectation of a right of access to all places at all times. In addition, the right of access does not extend to use of motor vehicles on private or estate roads.

Seasonal restrictions
Red and sika deer stalking:
Stags: 1 July to 20 October
Hinds: 21 October to 15 February
Deer may be culled at other times for welfare reasons. The seasons for fallow and roe deer (less common) are also longer. Many estates belong to the Hillphones Network which provides advance notice of shoots.
Grouse shooting:
12 August to 10 December
Forestry: Felling: all year
Planting: November to May
Heather burning:
September to April
Lambing:
March to May (dogs should be kept on a lead at all times near livestock)

CAUTION
Otters Crossing

From Arran in the south to Coll in the north, the islands in this section each have a distinctive character, landscape and language, with Gaelic culture very much alive and well. The area's wildlife is as varied as the islands themselves and can provide some magical encounters: it is rare to come quite so close to a wild-eyed stag as is possible on Arran and Jura, while the puffins that nest on the Treshnish Isles are famously approachable.

The islands also play a vital role in supporting some of Scotland's most spectacular and vulnerable species. Islay is home to huge gatherings of wintering geese; the machair habitat on Coll, Tiree and Colonsay is synonymous with the endangered corncrake and chough; while Mull holds important populations of golden and white-tailed sea eagles – the latter now expanding its range following reintroduction.

And the marine life of the Hebrides is no less impressive: otters flourish along the food-rich shores, while whales, dolphins and basking sharks are all seen in summer months. The smaller islands are perfect for exploring unaided, while the area is particularly well served by professional wildlife operators offering guided trips around the larger islands and surrounding waters.

COLL
Tobermory
TIREE
MULL
Oban
COLONSAY
JURA
Bowmore
ISLAY
ARRAN
Brodick

8
7
6
5
4
3
2
1

Arran and the Argyll Islands

Arran

Getting there By ferry from Ardrossan.
Summer sailings (April-Oct) from Claonaig
(Kintyre) OS Map Landranger 69

Arran's popularity as a wildlife-watching destination continues to grow – particularly in the rugged north of the island.

As one of the most southerly and accessible of Scotland's islands, Arran is a justifiably popular destination, particularly with golfers and walkers.

Much of the island's appeal can be attributed to its unique geology. The Highland Boundary Fault that passes through its centre has made Arran a magnet for geologists, but is also responsible for the island's split personality: while the north is as remote and rugged as anywhere in the Highlands, the south is dominated by rolling moorland and fertile farmland. In between is Brodick, the island's main town and a

good starting point for exploring the wildlife that now also draws increasing visitors to Arran.

Brodick Bay itself is an important feeding ground for shorebirds, such as heron, shelduck and eider, while the rocks around Merkland Point are one of several haul-out sites for common seals around the island. The animals are visible just offshore from between the small jetty at the north of the bay and the entrance to Brodick Castle.

The castle's extensive grounds are also worth exploring. Ranger-led walks in summer provide interpretation on the exotic plant and tree life, while the gardens are home to many of the red squirrels that thrive on Arran in the absence of greys.

Nearby, the String Road heads inland across sweeping moorland that holds red-throated diver, short-eared owl and a significant population of breeding hen

Rigours of the rut

Well-conditioned hinds come into oestrus in September – the trigger for mature stags to leave their bachelor herds and attempt to corral and defend a group of hinds against all comers. They will do so by bellowing their ownership, sizing up competitors through parallel walking and even locking horns in a test of strength. Successful stags will mate with up to 20 hinds. The rut normally peaks in early to mid-October, although it can extend into November – by which time many stags are shadows of their former selves. The animals do not eat during this period and can lose up to 15 per cent of their body weight.

harrier. Look out, too, for golden eagle, which can often be seen hunting over the moor if travelling between North Sannox and Lochranza.

However, the most numerous of Arran's wildlife are the 2000 or so red deer that are largely contained in the northern half of the island by a lengthy deer fence. The village of Lochranza – a good base for exploring much of the north – is renowned for the hinds that regularly bask on the shingle by the ruined castle.

During the October rut, Lochranza can become a battleground as stags come down from the hills to claim and defend groups of

hinds. It is not unusual when driving around the village at this time to come face to face with a wild-eyed stag by the side of the road.

Many visitors to Lochranza also make the trek to the Cock of Arran (a 12km round trip from the castle) which provides a window not only onto some of Arran's most distinguished geological features – including Hutton's famous 'Unconformity' – but also the island's marine life. Minke whale, bottlenose dolphin and basking shark are all spotted with regularity during summer months, both here and further down the east coast.

◀ Loch Ranza at low tide

Islay

Getting there By ferry from Kennacraig
(Kintyre). Flights from Glasgow
OS Map Landranger 60

Famed for its wintering geese, rare choughs and raptors, Islay is a bird-watching destination for all seasons.

Blessed with so much rich, low-lying agricultural land, it is no surprise that farming has moulded the Islay landscape – the result being that the island's abundant wildlife relies heavily on farmland and other managed habitats.

Islay's bird life, in particular, is as accessible as it is diverse: it is not unusual to spot 50 species in a single day, while keen-eyed birders will more likely double that, particularly in spring.

Much of the action centres on the RSPB reserve at Loch Gruinart. The reserve, a working farm, was established to manage the thousands of barnacle and white-fronted geese that arrive from Greenland each autumn to enjoy Islay's mild winters. The geese roost mainly around the heads of Loch Gruinart and Loch Indaal, but disperse widely during the day to feed. Fields of wary birds can be encountered almost anywhere between October and late March.

The visitor facilities at Loch Gruinart include a hide, a short woodland trail and an observation room that provides panoramic views over the wet grassland. Here, a system of sluices and pipe drains helps create suitable conditions not only for wintering geese, but also breeding waders in spring. Lapwing, snipe and redshank all need a combination of marshy ground for feeding and drier areas for nesting.

Like the waders, the plump brown hares that dot many of the fields benefit from an absence of foxes on Islay, but do not have it all their own way. The island holds good numbers of peregrine falcon and golden

◀ Wetland at the head of Loch Gruinart

eagle, while hen harriers have enjoyed a particular renaissance. With more than 22 breeding pairs, Islay is second only to Orkney for numbers of this once heavily persecuted bird of prey.

Islay also lays claim to 85 per cent of the Scottish chough population, with the remainder on Colonsay and Oronsay. Choughs thrive on coastal habitat grazed by livestock – with insect-rich cow dung a reliable food source in winter – while the island's many deserted buildings provide welcome roost sites. The fields and dunes around the derelict Kilchoman Church at

Machir Bay are an excellent spot to observe these aerial acrobats.

In addition to Loch Gruinart, the RSPB operates two lower-key sites on Islay: the clifftop Oa reserve in the southwest of the island – another good area for chough – and the even less developed Smaull Farm (in the northwest). Visitors to the latter should seek information at Loch Gruinart.

For those preferring an expert guided tour of Islay's bird life, the excellent Islay Birding offers daytrips – plus multi-day bushcraft expeditions – from its base in Port Charlotte.

Barnacle geese feed in tight groups

Flights of fancy

The dawn and dusk flights of Islay's wintering geese can be truly spectacular, with up to 70 per cent (30,000) of the world's Greenland barnacle geese and 40 per cent (13,000) of the Greenland white-fronted goose populations on the island at any one time. During the day, there are particularly good views of feeding geese on the grassland between the heads of Loch Indaal and Loch Gruinart, while the observation area near the RSPB visitor centre is a perfect place to watch skeins of geese come in to roost at dusk.

Jura

Getting there **By ferry from Port Askaig, Islay. Private operators from Crinan harbour (Gemini Cruises) and Easdale (Sea.fari Adventures Oban)**
OS Map **Landranger 61**

Rugged and with large tracts of uninhabited land, the wild island of Jura is known for its thousands of red deer.

Separated from Islay by just a narrow sound, Jura is nonetheless a very different animal to its fertile neighbour. Not easily suited to agriculture, Jura was often ignored by early colonisers and retains a sense of isolation even today.

The name Jura is often said to originate from a Norse word meaning 'island of deer', although the excellent Feolin Cultural Centre (near the ferry slipway) argues otherwise. Regardless of accuracy, the moniker is apt: stalking is a mainstay of the economy and the island's 5,500 red deer heavily outnumber Jura's 150 or so year-round human inhabitants.

Deer can be found almost anywhere, including Feolin where the animals come down to the beach to feed on seaweed. Excellent swimmers, they have been known to swim across to both Islay and Scarba in the north.

The harsh environment means that Jura's deer carry less weight than those on the mainland, although they are of purer stock, with none of the hybridisation with introduced sika deer now found on the mainland.

The animals are visible year round, although the stags make their presence felt

Deer can be encountered almost anywhere on Jura

particularly loudly during the October rut. They include a handful of Cromie stags that exhibit a swept back antler formation that is unique to the island.

Jura is served by a single public road that winds up the east coast passing through Craighouse, the island's only village. The harbour is a good area for otters, as well as a favourite haul-out site for common seals.

The largely uninhabited north end is the site of Barnhill, the farmhouse where George Orwell wrote much of 1984. It is here that Jura's many raptors can best be appreciated; hen harrier and buzzard numbers are high, while there is a stable population of golden eagles. White-tailed sea eagles can also be seen, particularly in winter.

Jura's west coast is wilder still, with a geologically rich landscape of raised beaches, caves and cliffs. It is a magnet for adventurous walkers, although such unforgiving backcountry should be taken seriously at any time of year. Hikers should also note that Jura's moorland contains one of Scotland's highest concentrations of adders, although the snakes are not easily seen.

Most visitors to Jura drive, but cycling is an option. It can be a tough 45km ride from Feolin to the end of the public road at Lealt, but the wildlife watching possibilities are outstanding. From the road end, it is a further 13km to the Corryvreckan viewpoint – although wildlife guide Mike Richardson offers a pick-up service as part of a programme of guided walks.

Beware the Corryvreckan

The narrow channel that separates Jura from the island of Scarba has a justifiably fearsome reputation. On a flood tide, powerful currents converge over an underwater pinnacle to create a series of dangerous eddies and drop offs – the infamous Corryvreckan whirlpool. On a strong autumn flood tide, and when whipped up by a westerly wind, the noise of the roaring water can be heard for several miles. The tidal races stir up fish supplies, attracting plunge-diving gannets and marine life such as harbour porpoise. Sea.fari Adventures offers RIB trips to the whirlpool from Easdale (near Oban) and links up with Mike Richardson for guided walks on north Jura.

Guided trips are available in Jura's isolated north end

Colonsay

Getting there **By ferry from Oban, Kennacraig and Port Askaig (Islay)** OS Map **Landranger 61**

Chough and corncrake are just two of the wildlife treasures found on the remote island of Colonsay.

Marooned in the outer Firth of Lorne some 24km south of Mull, Colonsay is one of the smallest and most remote of the inhabited Hebridean islands.

But while modest in size – just 12km long and 3km wide – the island is blessed with a huge variety of terrain: high crags loom over raised beaches, while heather moorland and patches of woodland give way to an often rugged coastline, softened by coves and beaches. Such diverse habitat, coupled with a mild climate,

ensures an impressive range of plant and animal life.

Ideal for exploration by bike, much of Colonsay is served by a single 'main' road with two spurs that head south to the Strand – a wide stretch of beach that connects with sister island Oronsay at low tide – and north past the exotic gardens at Colonsay House.

Squeezed between the two highest points on the island, the crescent-shaped beach at Kiloran Bay is a dominant feature in the north. Nearby, the sea cliffs that run south from Uragaig hold thousands of breeding seabirds, with particularly high numbers of fulmar, kittiwake and guillemot. The cliffs here feel the full force of the Atlantic and have been fractured into a series of caves and archways around Port nam Fluachan.

Choughs feeding along the shoreline

Chough central

Oronsay and the Balnahard dunes on Colonsay are among the best places in Scotland to see chough – a distinctive member of the crow family with its red bill and legs. Now an extremely localised breeder, the entire Scottish population (around 90 pairs) is concentrated here and on nearby Islay. Preferring areas of short pasture with soil soft enough to probe for invertebrates, chough thrive where low-intensity livestock farming is still practiced. Winter flocks of 50-plus birds can be seen on Colonsay and Oronsay, as well as non-breeding flocks of around 30 birds in summer.

To the north, a farm track continues past Kiloran Bay through prime golden eagle territory on its way to the sheltered coves of Balnahard Bay. Shelduck, oystercatcher and flocks of rare chough can all be seen here, while not surprisingly there are also plenty of eider ducks – known in Gaelic as 'lach Cholasaidh', or Colonsay duck.

Equally picturesque, the south of the island is characterised by yet more coves and outlying skerries that are favourite haul outs for grey seals. The animals are often seen off the Ardskenish peninsula and around Rubh' an Dunain – their eerie calls sometimes drifting on the wind.

Oronsay is also well used by seals. Managed by the RSPB as a nature reserve, the island is farmed with wildlife very much in mind. As a result, it is another hotspot for chough, with a breeding pair near the island's ruined Augustinian priory, while corncrake also nest in the nettle beds each summer.

Access to Oronsay is tide dependent: while a spring tide allows around two hours either side of low water to walk across and back, neap tides leave the Strand closed to anyone without a kayak. Check at Scalasaig pier for tide times and possible boat trips around the island.

◀ The lighthouse guarding Scalasaig harbour

Mull

Getting there **By ferry from Oban, Lochaline (Morvern) and Kilchoan (Ardnamurchan)** OS Maps **Landranger 47, 48 and 49**

Mountainous Mull boasts one of the best year-round concentrations of land and marine life anywhere in Scotland.

A paradise for wildlife watchers, Mull is the place to come for close encounters with otters, golden eagles and white-tailed sea eagles – collectively the island's 'big three'. According to the season, there are also boundless opportunities to see red deer, seals and a host of waders and divers around the sea lochs.

Although a year-round wildlife-watching destination, spring and early summer are particularly good times to visit: the island's fickle weather can be at its most settled, wild flowers are coming into bloom and many species can be seen displaying, breeding and defending territories.

Of the big three species, the main road through Glen More – particularly around the Three Lochs area – offers a good chance of spotting a golden eagle as it intersects the territories of several pairs. Keep an eye out for birds breaking the skyline above the hills.

Sea eagles, meanwhile, prefer rocky coastlines and are often seen around Loch Don and the fringes of Loch na Keal. The best option, however, is to visit the purpose-built hide at Loch Frisa which provides a carefully managed, and rare, opportunity to view the UK's largest bird of prey at the nest. The hide is open from April to July if the eagles are

Sea eagles on show

Having been wiped out in Scotland in the early 1900s, the white-tailed sea eagle was successfully reintroduced on Rum in 1975 and first bred on Mull in 1985. Although hindered by the continued threat of egg theft, accidental poisoning and a low reproductive rate, the birds have enjoyed a gradual recovery, with more than 30 pairs now nesting on the west coast of Scotland. Several pairs hold territories on Mull, with the Loch Frisa birds the focus of the world's first dedicated sea eagle viewing hide. While on Mull, look for the birds soaring above rocky coastlines on huge, 'fingered' wings – their sheer size obvious when mobbed by gulls and crows.

Sea eagles have a wingspan of up to 2.5m

nesting and visits must be booked in advance.

During the breeding season, volunteers from the local community work with police, RSPB and the Forestry Commission as part of Mull Eagle Watch – a 24-hour initiative that protects the island's eagles from egg thieves and general disturbance.

Otters, meanwhile, are harder to pinpoint: they are quite nomadic and territories can span several kilometres. Traditionally, the north shore of Loch na Keal towards Ulva Ferry has offered good sightings, as have areas around Calgary and Croggan. Move slowly along the shore, keeping an eye just offshore, particularly on sheltered and calm sections of sea lochs. Otters also like to follow the tide

in as they hunt for crabs and butterfish.

Further out to sea, the nutrient rich waters, naturally warmed by a tributary of the Gulf Stream, support an array of marine life. The summer months bring minke whales to their regular feeding grounds and sometimes orcas. Smaller cetaceans such as common, bottlenose and Risso's dolphins, as well as harbour porpoise, are also plentiful.

A good option is to join one of Mull's excellent land or marine wildlife tour operators. Many run trips year round with marine organisations such as Sea Life Surveys in Tobermory combining wildlife watching with serious scientific research.

◀ Mull from Staffa

Treshnish Isles

Getting there **Turus Mara operate daily sailings (Easter-Oct) from Ulva Ferry, Mull**
OS Map **Landranger 48**

Easily visited from Mull, the Treshnish Isles offer an enticing mix of wildlife, cultural history and splendid isolation.

An uninhabited island chain, the Treshnish Isles are a familiar sight off the west coast of Mull. With eight main islands of varying size stretching for 11km north to south, the archipelago is often said to resemble a line of distant battleships.

Ruined fortifications on the most northerly of the islands, plus an abandoned settlement on the main island of Lunga, are indications of past habitation. Today, however, these fertile islands are owned by the Hebridean Trust and serve as an undisturbed haven for a variety of wildlife – including around 60 species of bird.

In autumn, the boulder beaches on the smaller islands are an important breeding ground for Atlantic grey seals – with around 1000 pups born each year – while the larger islands provide good winter grazing for small numbers of barnacle geese

However, it is in spring and summer that the Treshnish Isles really come alive as thousands of seabirds return to the islands to breed. Lunga is very much the centre of activity with around 1600 pairs of puffin, plus large numbers of kittiwake, fulmar, shag and guillemot.

Puffins at rest

Although visible around much of Lunga, the highest concentrations of seabirds are found on Dun Chruit (or Harp Rock), an isolated pillar on the west of the island that literally crawls with tightly packed guillemots.

Several boat operators provide trips to the islands, with the long-established Turus Mara, based at Ulva Ferry on Mull, the closest. There is no landing area as such on Lunga; instead, visitors are transported by pontoon onto the boulder beach, from where it is a short walk to Harp Rock.

The grassy banks alongside the path are riddled with puffin burrows and the birds are often quite tolerant. Listen for their soft growling in and around the burrows, although be careful not to stray too close: puffin burrows stretch up to two metres underground and are easily crushed by careless feet.

Back on the shore, the boulder beaches that appear silent and empty during the day provide ideal nest sites for hundreds of storm petrels. These secretive seabirds feed far out at sea during the day and only return to their nest chambers at night to avoid predation by gulls and skuas.

While travelling to and from the islands, keep an eye out for marine life. Seals – both common and grey – are a constant feature around the skerries, while the waters nearby have traditionally been a good area for minke whale and basking shark.

Sound of music

Boat trips to the Treshnish Isles often include a visit to the nearby island of Staffa – home to Fingal's Cave, a geological phenomenon immortalised by the composer Mendelssohn in his *Hebrides Overture*. A legacy of Staffa's volcanic past, this huge sea cave is formed from multi-sided blocks of basalt that rise dramatically out of the sea. Easily accessed along a rock platform, the cave is an impressive site, despite the summer crowds. While on Staffa, it is worth also exploring the paths that criss-cross the island above the cave: a handful of puffins and great skuas nest around the island, while the views back to Mull can be spectacular.

◄ Harp Rock on Lunga

Tiree

Getting there By ferry from Oban. Flights from Glasgow OS Map Landranger 46

A long tradition of low-intensity farming has turned this sun-blessed island into the corncrake capital of Scotland.

With its fertile land, long hours of sunshine and mild winters, it is no wonder that Tiree has attracted settlers since the Iron Age. However, it is the action of the island's more recent crofting communities that have contributed most to its array of wildlife.

Although Tiree has only a smattering of land mammals, it has an abundance of marine and bird life. Grey and common seals bask in favoured spots, while bottlenose dolphins and basking sharks can be spotted on calm summer days, particularly around Gunna Sound.

Meanwhile, the traditional use of seaweed to fertilise the land has created swathes of glorious machair – a distinctive habitat that, in spring, is as noisy as it is colourful when lapwing, snipe and other waders display crazily above the meadows.

Elsewhere, the island's shallow lochs and wetland areas are home to a variety of ducks, as well as wintering whooper swans and thousands of geese, while the cliffs at

The elusive corncrake

Ceann a' Mharra hold significant seabird colonies in summer.

In ornithological terms, however, the island is best known as the summer home of over a quarter of the UK's population of corncrake – an idiosyncratic species that arrives from its sub-Saharan wintering grounds in late April.

Although a shy bird that craves the cover of dense vegetation, the male nonetheless possesses a rasping call that often continues long into the night. Such is its incessant racket that the bird has gained many names in Gaelic, including 'cleabhair caoch' (or nutty noisemaker). The birds are best seen early in the season when the grass is still relatively short and males are establishing territories.

Now confined to isolated areas of the Highlands and islands, the corncrake has been the subject of a huge conservation effort. Inherently vulnerable because of its short lifespan – three years at best – the bird has suffered greatly from modern farming methods.

However, considerable progress has been made thanks to a range of agri-environment schemes in which crofters are encouraged to use 'corncrake-friendly' farming techniques, such as leaving areas of cover during spring and cutting crops later in the year to give chicks extra time to fledge. Participating crofters also cut fields from the inside out, allowing the birds room for escape. The crofters, whose silage can suffer loss of quality from late cutting, are reimbursed with payments from the schemes.

The efforts appear to be working: in 2005, there were 310 calling males on Tiree – the highest number since surveys began.

Just 19km in length and largely flat, the island is perfect for exploring by bike. Listening to a rasping corncrake against a backdrop of Tiree's big sky and seemingly endless seascape is a quintessentially Hebridean experience.

Surf's up

Tiree is not only one of the sunniest places in Britain, but also one of its windiest – ideal for water sports enthusiasts. Not surprisingly, the island has become a mecca for windsurfers and hosts the annual UK wavesailing championship. Expert boarders can enjoy the uninterrupted swells off the Atlantic from almost any of the beaches, while beginners can find their feet in the shallow waters of Loch Bhasapol.

◂ Tiree has some of the finest machair in the Hebrides

Coll

Getting there By ferry from Oban or via Tiree OS Map Landranger 46

Quirky wildlife, glorious machair and white sand beaches combine to make Coll one of the most beguiling of the Hebridean islands.

As on neighbouring Tiree, traditional low-intensity farming methods have combined with enriching windblown sand to support an outstanding variety of life on Coll. The island is of huge botanical interest with 11 types of orchid alone and literally hundreds of other flowering plants on the machair.

The RSPB is now one of Coll's largest landowners with the Totronald reserve and visitor information room at the west end of the island a good starting point for any exploration. It is here that designated areas have been given over to corncrake.

Although Coll cannot match the excellent lowland habitat found on Tiree, the island's corncrake population nonetheless continues to flourish, with around 150 calling males.

Many of the island's farmers now see the value in farming with corncrake in mind and an agri-environment approach has been adopted almost island-wide. As such, hay meadows and overgrown areas in field corners should be avoided during the breeding season.

Although present from late April until September, this is one bird that is more likely to be heard than seen: the males call long into the night, although they generally quieten down towards the end of July.

But Coll is not just about corncrakes or even the RSPB reserve: the whole island is a joy to explore and offers important habitat for many different plants and animals. The moorland and machair support healthy

◀ Hogh Bay on Coll

Machair marvel

The distinctive Hebridean machair (pronounced *mach-err*) owes its roots to traditional farming methods. Crofters have long used seaweed as a natural fertiliser on soils already enriched by lime-rich windblown shell sand and subsequent livestock grazing. The result is a mosaic of orchids, corn marigolds, wild pansies and many other flowering plants that colour the meadows in patterns of yellows, reds and pinks between May and August.

numbers of breeding waders, while the colourful shelduck often nests in abandoned rabbit burrows. Red-throated divers make use of Coll's many inland lochans while, in winter, barnacle, greylag and white-fronted geese are all present in high numbers.

Other species include two nationally rare bees – the great yellow bumblebee and a mining bee – as well as some genuine oddities: the world's largest herd of Eriskay ponies, multi-horned Hebridean sheep and deer-like soays that are descended from Viking sheep.

In addition, Coll's rugged coastline holds a good population of otters, with Feall Bay, around Arinagour pier and Sorisdale in the north of the island all good places to sit patiently and watch. The clear waters also offer an excellent chance of seeing a basking shark – a gentle giant that has become increasingly plentiful in Hebridean waters in recent summers.

Recreational divers, meanwhile, enjoy the dense kelp forests, abundance of soft corals and numerous wrecks that dot these waters. Perhaps the most famous is the Nevada, which sank in 1942 on her way to Africa and whose mast was visible above the water until the 1970s.

Redshank – one of many breeding waders on Coll

23

Skye is a haven for three of Scotland's most sought after species: otters, golden eagles and the even larger white-tailed sea eagle. Seeing such wildlife anywhere is a thrill, but to do so against the backdrop of Skye's dramatic landscape only adds to the experience.

Of this chapter's three entries on Skye, two provide general tips on the habitat – and conditions – to consider when searching for these far-ranging species. A third is more location specific: the mouth of Loch Coruisk, home to a large colony of common seals and gateway to Skye's fabled Cuillin ridge.

This section continues with an adventure on nearby Raasay, an island often overlooked by the crowds that flock to Skye, before heading south to the Small Isles – a collection of four islands dominated by Rum with a bruising Cuillin of its own. Site of the successful reintroduction of sea eagles in the 1970s, Rum is also home to a remarkable hilltop colony of Manx shearwaters.

By comparison, Canna, Eigg and Muck are very small isles indeed, but that just makes them easier to explore. Just be sure to keep an eye out for marine life when travelling between them.

Skye, Raasay and the Small Isles

Kylerhea Forestry Commission Scotland

Getting there **Signposted from A850, 6km west of the Skye bridge, or by ferry (May-Aug) from Glenelg (Kintail)**
OS Maps **Landranger 32 and 33**

Kylerhea otter haven is one of several places on Skye to sit quietly and try to spot the island's most charismatic but elusive – mammal.

While the roadbridge at Kyle of Lochalsh now provides a grand gateway to Skye, taking the summer car ferry across the narrows from Glenelg can be an equally memorable way of reaching the island. Ferry users also have the benefit of disembarking close to the Kylerhea otter haven – a Forestry Commission initiative designed to highlight the kind of habitat that makes Skye such a hotspot for otters.

The haven is reached along a 1km path that ends in a hide perched high above the Kylerhea narrows. This is prime otter territory, with an undisturbed stretch of beach and a tumbling freshwater burn leading into various man-made pools – constructed to encourage favourite prey items such as frogs.

Otters are large animals, with males reaching up to 1.2m in length, but they can still be difficult to spot in the water; often the only sign is the head and a trailing ripple. They are, however, unmistakeable once on land with their arched backs and loping gait.

But, as elsewhere on Skye, there can be no guarantees at Kylerhea. Skye's coastal otters are active by day, but it still takes a keen eye, or just good fortune, to spot a wary animal with a home range that extends for many kilometres. Unsuccessful visitors should certainly not be discouraged. Skye is one of the best places in Scotland for otters, with some 350 individuals out of a total population of around 6600.

The south of Skye, in particular, is blessed with several good areas for otter watching – thanks in part to the underlying geology.

◀ The entrance to Kylerhea otter haven.

The non porous Torridonian sandstone that dominates much of the Sleat peninsula allows fresh water to collect in pools above the high tide mark, which are in turn used by otters to wash salt from their fur. Such cleansing is essential for maintaining the thermal insulation of the animals' coats.

In addition to Kylerhea, try the Kyleakin slipway (at dawn or dusk), between the shore and the island at Dun Sgathaich castle (Sleat), or along the roadside at Faoilean on the way to Elgol (Strathaird). The latter is a particularly good place to park up and sit quietly. Another good spot is Broadford pier, while continuing along the coast towards Irishman's Point can also reap rewards.

The International Otter Survival Fund (IOSF) – a conservation organisation based in Broadford – would be interested to hear about all sightings, which can be reported via its website (www.otter.org).

Otter watching

Otters have an uncanny knack of appearing when least expected, but sharp-eyed observers can also increase their chance of spotting the animals by first identifying signs of their presence. Fresh spraint (dark coloured droppings) left in prominent places, remains of prey items and footprints (with five toes and clear webbing in between) are all good indicators of recent otter activity. But remember: although short sighted, otters are experts at detecting movement. Fortunately, they dive regularly when foraging offshore, allowing around 20 seconds for observers to shift position or reach for a camera.

Skye's eagles

Getting there Via Skye bridge at Kyle
of Lochalsh or by ferry from Mallaig and
Glenelg (May-Aug) OS Maps Landranger
32 and 23

**Skye offers a rare chance to catch sight
of Scotland's two largest birds of prey –
sometimes even sharing the same
thermals.**

Although Mull is more often referred to as
'Eagle Island', the Isle of Skye is no less
deserving of such a moniker. Appropriately
enough given the grandeur of the
landscape, Skye is a wonderful destination
for enjoying golden and white-tailed sea
eagles – two potent symbols of Scotland's
wild places.

As with so many raptors, both have
endured a long history of human
persecution and it is only recently that the
golden eagle has clawed its way back to
stability. The sea eagle, meanwhile, is now
making a gradual comeback following
reintroduction.

Scotland now holds around 430 pairs of
golden eagle, with the Hebridean islands an
increasingly important centre for the
species. However, with more than 30 pairs
holding territories on the island, Skye
supports higher densities than most.

Although the birds nest on inaccessible
crags, such habitat can be found across a
range of territory on Skye – even down to
sea level in places. As such, golden eagles
can be seen from almost any road on
the island.

Eagles are often best spotted on a clear
day with a slight breeze: be patient and
keep an eye on the skyline. Spring can be a
particularly active time, although don't
discount winter either: the short days mean

Celtic collaboration

Skye's golden eagles have provided valuable donor stock as part of a scheme to reintroduce the species to the hill country of Donegal in northwest Ireland. Since the initiative began in 2000, around 20 chicks have been taken under licence from Scottish nests for release. Most are taken from nests that contain two chicks, a situation that in the wild usually sees the death of the weaker chick. It will take time, however, to gauge the success of the reintroduction: many young eagles struggle to survive their first winter and do not usually breed until at least four years old.

Golden eagle on carrion

less time to hunt and eagles can be more easily spotted. On the Sleat peninsula, try the loop road around Tarskavaig and Ord, while a walk to Camasunary in the heart of the Cuillin or along the Trotternish ridge often gives good views.

And the chances of spotting a golden eagle sharing the same air space as its even larger cousin are ever increasing. Once the dominant species on Skye before being wiped out in the 1900s, the sea eagle has begun to repopulate the island. Skye currently holds around 25 per cent (eight or nine pairs) of Scotland's breeding population, although with 1000km of prime coastal habitat there is scope for many more.

After some initial conflict, the two species have established their largely separate niches and are now more accepting of one another. While the golden eagle shows more attachment to the land, the sea eagle is predominantly a coastal species, with a corresponding diet that is heavy on fish and seabirds.

Boat trips that sail into good sea eagle territory are available from Portree and Broadford, while a walk along the Scorrybreck path to Black Rock on the north shore of Loch Portree is also worthwhile. Elsewhere, in Dunvegan, try a walk to MacLeod's Maidens on the west shore of Loch Bracadale. Another option is the nearby Aros Centre, which operates a CCTV link to a nearby eyrie (March-Oct).

◀ The Trotternish ridge – fine golden eagle country.

Loch Coruisk and the Cuillin

Getting there Boats from Elgol, Strathaird
(April-Oct) OS Map Landranger 32

**A journey to the enigmatic Loch Coruisk,
home to a colony of common seals and
gateway to Scotland's most celebrated
mountain ridge.**

Skye's sawtooth Cuillin ridge can be
approached from many directions, but one
of the finest ways in is by sea. Sailing from
Elgol across Loch Scavaig and into the
narrows below the mouth of Loch Coruisk
not only provides a dramatic introduction to
these bruising mountains, but also affords
close views of a colony of common seals
resident year round at the base of the cliffs.

This is perfect habitat for common seals –
one of only two species found in Scottish
waters. While their cousins, the larger greys,
prefer more exposed coasts and skerries,
commons frequent sheltered sea lochs and
sandy estuaries.

Scotland holds roughly 30,000 common
seals out of a world population of around half
a million. Colonies were hit in the 1980s by
the highly contagious phocine distemper
virus (PDV) in an epidemic that swept
through northern Europe. The virus
reappeared in 2002 and took its toll once
more, with common seals curiously much
more susceptible to PDV than greys.

Today, however, the Loch Coruisk colony
appears in rude health with a population of
up to 200 animals.

The seals give birth to a single pup in May
or June and summer visitors will see plenty

common seal with pup

Spot the difference

When in the water, it can be hard to tell the difference between common and grey seals. However, common seals have a more dog-like head and v-shaped nostrils, while greys have a longer muzzle and parallel nostrils. Once on land, the distinctions are clearer: common seals are much smaller than greys and have a more uniform spotted coat. The biggest difference, however, is in pupping time: commons give birth in summer and greys in the autumn.

of pups hauled out on the rocks with their mothers. Unlike greys, common seal pups are born with adult colouring and can accompany their mothers into the water almost from birth.

Loch Coruisk itself sits above and separated from the sea by the tumbling River Scavaig, just a short walk from the jetty at the head of Loch na Cuilce. A rough and boggy path leads walkers around the loch and deep into the imposing mountains. Otters are sometimes seen at the margins of river and sea, while red deer are often seen at the shoreline, grazing the seaweed for nutrients.

The *Bella Jane* operates daily trips from Elgol (April to Oct) and by special arrangement out of season. For maximum time ashore, take the first boat in and the last one out. Some walkers take the boat one way and hike back along the coast. However, the return to Elgol involves negotiating the Bad Step, an imposing rock slab that requires caution and nerve.

While on the water, scan for signs of cetacean activity. Manx shearwaters from Rum also gather in large numbers, particularly in the autumn, while basking sharks are another feature of these waters. It was on nearby Soay that Gavin Maxwell operated his short-lived basking shark factory before becoming better known as a naturalist and author of *Ring of Bright Water*.

◀ Loch Coruisk

Raasay

Getting there By ferry from Sconser, Skye
OS Map Landranger 24

Although just a short hop from Skye, the often overlooked island of Raasay has a very different flavour — and plenty of undisturbed wildlife.

Sinuous and sparsely populated, Raasay occupies a striking position between Skye and the Applecross peninsula. With its rugged coastline and peppering of tiny islands in the north, Raasay is a treat for more intrepid wildlife explorers.

In pre-Clearance times, much of the population lived along the east coast, although all that remains today are the ruined townships at Hallaig and Screapadal – poignant reminders of a sad chapter in history immortalised by the work of Raasay poet Sorley MacLean.

Today, most of the island's residents live in the south around the wooded confines of Inverarish, a village originally built to house German prisoners-of-war that mined the island's supply of iron ore during WWI.

Inverarish aside, Raasay is wild in appearance. Much of the island can be explored from the public road that heads north as far as Arnish, with several paths heading into more remote areas. Wildlife can be encountered almost anywhere.

The south coast from the pier to Inverarish and to the lighthouse at Eyre Point can be a good area for otters, particularly early or late in the day. For a more strenuous outing, try the rough route

Marine acrobat

The common dolphin is best recognised by its colouring, with a yellow tinged hourglass pattern on its flanks that stands out against a dark back and creamy-white chest. It also has a long, thin beak. One of the most abundant cetaceans worldwide, common dolphins live in highly social groups and are often found in deeper Scottish waters during summer months. The animals are not only boisterous and acrobatic – frequently 'bow-riding' in the wake of boats – but also extremely vocal, with their high-pitched squealing sometimes heard above the water.

along the east coast from the road end at North Fearns to the ruined 15th-century castle at Brochel (16km).

Not many people pass this way and the path can be gruelling, but it is an atmospheric trek heavy with the weight of island history. Golden eagle, buzzard and raven are all present around the inland cliffs, while seals haul out on the skerries below the castle. If feeling fit, take a detour to the summit of Dun Caan, a curious basalt cap that marks the highest point on the island (443m).

The north of Raasay is more remote still with areas of rough grazing interspersed with rocky outcrops and isolated lochans. This is good territory for red deer and the occasional

sea eagle that drifts across from Skye.

Beyond Arnish, clear tracks head further north through birch woodland to the kyles of Fladda (2.0km) and Rona (8km) – the largest of Raasay's offshore islands. The whole coastline here is a wonderful area for otters, seals and other marine life: common dolphin and basking shark both feed in the sound during summer months.

The island of Fladday can be reached on foot at low tide, but access to Rona requires a boat. Ask at Raasay House Outdoor Centre in Clachan for details. The centre, which offers accommodation as well as a variety of sailing, walking and kayaking adventures, can also advise on the condition of the island's more remote paths.

◀ Raasay's east coast near Hallaig.

Rum Scottish Natural Heritage

Getting there **By ferry from Mallaig (year round) and Arisaig (May-Sept). Private RIB charters available from Mallaig and Elgol, Skye** OS Map **Landranger 39**

Blessed with dramatic mountain scenery – a magnet for walkers and geologists – Rum has immense wildlife appeal, including red deer and a vast hilltop colony of Manx shearwaters.

For many day-trippers, the island of Rum is all about Kinloch Castle – a gloriously opulent building completed in 1901 for the enjoyment of George Bullough, the son of a Lancastrian textile magnate.

Once off limits, the island is now managed as a National Nature Reserve by Scottish Natural Heritage (SNH) and visitors are encouraged to sample not just the castle, but also Rum's many natural wonders.

Often dubbed Scotland's 'outdoor laboratory', Rum is an important centre of conservation work and wildlife research. After two failed attempts elsewhere, white-tailed sea eagles were released on Rum between 1975 and 1985 as part of a successful reintroduction programme. Today, around 30 pairs have reclaimed past haunts along the west coast of Scotland, while one to two pairs continue to breed on Rum.

The island has also been the focus of extensive research on red deer, with a long-running population study examining the interaction between the herd and its environment. The results have formed the basis for deer management across Scotland for many years. Not surprisingly, Rum is an excellent place to view these animals, with the deer around the main study area at Kilmory particularly tame.

Elsewhere, high in the Rum Cuillin, walkers are often intrigued by the many burrows that

Manx shearwater chick

Shearwater predation

By seabird standards, the breeding season for Manx shearwaters is a lengthy one: usually, a single egg is laid in mid May and chicks fledge in August or September. Some are lost to golden eagles and ravens, while there have been more unusual reports of red deer eating the heads and legs of chicks as a source of calcium to promote antler growth. Of much more concern, however, are early signs of brown rat predation of eggs – a worrying discovery with potentially devastating consequences for the Rum colony.

stud the hillsides. However, there are no rabbits on Rum; instead, the burrows are home to a vast colony of Manx shearwaters, thought to number more than 100,000 pairs, or a third of the world population.

Built for life at sea and hopelessly defenceless on land, Manx shearwaters find Rum's remote mountaintops perfect for their needs. Rum's geology is also favourable with the loose peridotite scree – deposited during the volcanic activity that formed the island – ideal for excavating burrows.

Feeding at sea during the day, the birds only brave a return to their burrows on the darkest of nights. Such was the din of returning birds that early Viking

settlers believed the hills to be the home of trolls – hence the name of mountains such as Trollaval.

SNH staff run guided walks in the summer, including night-time visits to the shearwater colony. Visitors are also welcome to explore the colony themselves, although the location and the birds' nocturnal habits point to obvious challenges. Camping near the main areas – the easiest to access being on the slopes of Hallival – can be the best option. August and September are particularly good months, with many non-breeding birds spending time on the guano-enriched grassland outside their burrows.

◀ Manx shearwater habitat high in the Rum Cuillin

Canna National Trust for Scotland

Getting there **By ferry from Mallaig (year round) and Arisaig (May–Sept).**
OS Map **Landranger 39**

Lonely Canna combines impressive seabird cliffs with the chance of spotting some of the area's diverse marine life.

The most westerly of the Small Isles, the relatively gentle profile of Canna stands in stark contrast to the rugged relief of neighbouring Rum. Sparsely populated and just 8km in length, Canna and its satellite island of Sanday lend themselves to leisurely exploration. With so little disturbance, the wildlife rewards can be great.

John Lorne Campbell, a renowned Gaelic scholar, owned the island from 1938 until 1981 when he gifted it to the National Trust for Scotland (NTS). Also a keen naturalist, Campbell treated Canna as a nature reserve and the NTS continues to closely monitor its bird life in addition to farming the island.

Canna holds important numbers of breeding seabirds, particularly on the cliffs to the north and east of the island. Sadly, a colony of Manx shearwaters that once topped 1000 pairs has been all but wiped out by brown rats. Other species such as puffin, fulmar, shag and razorbill are also in decline, with rat predation again a major factor.

A shark's tale

Basking sharks inhabit temperate waters all over the world and start to appear around western coasts of Britain from May. These impressive fish are now appearing with increasing regularity in Scottish waters, most likely due to the movement north of favourite prey items such as copepods – a warm water and highly nutritious type of animal plankton. Since 2003, the Scottish Wildlife Trust has participated in a UK-wide basking shark survey that has used photo-identification and video-recording techniques to create a database of known individuals. Other studies have even used satellite tagging to follow the sharks' movements outside the summer months.

Having recently gained funding, the NTS is now taking action: it has recruited a specialist company from New Zealand to exterminate the island's estimated 10,000 brown rats. It is hoped that once the rats have been eradicated, seabirds will begin to return, with the large Manx shearwater presence on Rum providing a potential ready source of juvenile birds.

In addition to seabirds, Canna's cliffs are also the haunt of golden eagles that work the thermals along the north coast. The area around Rubha Langanais is a particularly good spot: in addition to eagles, grey and common seals haul out on the skerries, while basking sharks feed close inshore during summer months – their tail and dorsal fins visible as they swim open-mouthed near the surface of the water.

Although the second largest fish in the world (up to 12m in length), relatively little is known about this plankton-feeding species. What is clear is that basking shark numbers off the west coast of Scotland have increased dramatically, with the waters around Canna as good a place as any to spot them. The ferry from Mallaig has even been known to pause at the mouth of the harbour to let larger specimens drift by.

With care, it is possible to enjoy many of Canna's key species by walking along the cliffs from Rubha Langanais to Compass Hill and An Coroghon (Prison Rock) at the eastern end of the island. Maps and information on wildlife sightings are available from the tearoom (open March-Oct) overlooking the harbour.

◀ The south side of Canna with Rum in the distance

Eigg

Getting there **By ferry from Mallaig (year round) and Arisaig (May-Sept)**
OS Map **Landranger 39**

Distinctive in both profile and ownership, Eigg includes some of the most varied landscape in the Small Isles.

Many visitors to Eigg explore the island between ferries, often including a sprint up An Sgurr, the dramatic ridge of pitchstone lava that presides over Galmisdale Bay. But although small – just 8km by 5.5km – visitors eager to savour the wildlife of this highly individual island require a little more time.

Much more than the other Small Isles, Eigg is characterised by areas of very different habitat: between An Sgurr in the south and the basalt cliffs of Cleadale in the north are stretches of fertile meadow, heather moorland and woodland – the

latter a legacy of planting that began in the 1860s.

As a result, Eigg has an unusually large population of woodland birds for such a small Hebridean island. The trails that lead through Manse Wood and other areas of tree cover highlight resident species such as buzzard, spotted flycatcher and goldcrest, plus a variety of migrants in spring.

Such habitat stands in contrast to the classic crofting landscape found beneath the Cleadale cliffs in the north. Traditionally farmed, Cleadale is a wonderful place for flowering plants, while the meadows also shelter snipe and the occasional corncrake in summer.

The coast here is easily explored with Laig Bay connected at low tide to Camus Sgiotaig – better known as Singing Sands because of the white quartz sand that squeaks underfoot. The views are spectacular with the formidable Rum Cuillin

◄ Eigg from the Rùm Cuillin

Taking control

In 1997, Eigg made headline news across Scotland when the local community (around 70 people) put an end to more than 150 years of often uncertain landlordism by buying their own island. Eigg residents joined with two partners, the Highland Council (the local authority) and the Scottish Wildlife Trust, to form the Isle of Eigg Heritage Trust – the first non-crofting buyout and first island to be bought in Scotland. In an instant, the community had a stake in its own future and was able to play a full role in all decisions affecting the economic development and conservation management of their island.

ever present in clear weather. Look out for red-throated diver offshore, while this is also a good stretch of coast for otters.

Eigg's crumbling cliffs mean that it holds the least number of breeding seabirds of all the Small Isles, although black guillemot nest amongst the fallen boulders and Manx shearwater inhabit inaccessible burrows near the top of the Ben Bhuide cliffs. Although unreachable, the birds can be heard returning from fishing trips around the Cleadale road on summer nights.

Meanwhile, the waters around Eigg – as elsewhere in the Small Isles – offer regular sightings of minke whale, porpoise and, increasingly, basking shark. Most reliable of all, however, are the seals (both common and grey) that haul out at either end of the island, including near the pier in Galmisdale Bay

Visitors are encouraged to explore as much of the island as possible: check in at the craft shop by the jetty for trail maps as well as details on weekly guided walks offered by the resident SWT warden (April to Sept).

Grey seals haul out around the island

Muck

Getting there **By ferry from Mallaig (year round) and Arisaig (May-Sept)** OS Map **Landranger 39**

Muck's coastline offers some of the finest seascapes in the Small Isles – often with the marine life to match.

Just 3km long, Muck is tiny even by Small Isle standards. Run entirely on wind power and with a population of around 30 people, the island fits most people's idea of an unhurried Hebridean idyll.

But although dwarfed by its neighbours, Muck's coastline and fertile interior have enough interest to keep visitors more than occupied. Many hours can pass exploring the island's cliffs, coves and skerries, with the wind turbine above the tiny settlement of Port Mor providing an almost constant landmark.

The island's name is said to come from the Gaelic 'muc', meaning pig, or 'muc mara' (sea pig, or porpoise) and the marine life can be as abundant as anywhere in the Small Isles. There is good sea watching along much of the coast, especially from vantage points such as Am Maol: as well as porpoise, lucky visitors in summer might even spot a minke whale or basking shark, particularly on calm days.

While exploring, look carefully around rocky coves for otter runs that head inland through the grass. Quite distinctive in places, with the grass curved over to form almost a complete tunnel, the runs are often marked with spraint at points along their length. Otters are present around the island, although Camas na Cairidh in the north – where it is possible to stay in a replica Mongolian yurt – is a particularly good area.

Elsewhere, the nearby skerries around Gallanach Bay are a favourite haul-out spot for grey seals. Opposite is the main farm on

◀ Gallanach Bay, Muck

Coastal and Marine National Park

Scotland is in the initial stages of creating the UK's first Coastal and Marine National Park – a move designed to safeguard the future of some of the country's most valuable coastal habitat and wildlife. Having launched a public consultation on the proposal in 2005, the Scottish Executive now has to decide how and where. It will be a difficult decision, with areas as far apart as Shetland, the Western Isles and the Moray coast all potentially vying for inclusion. Expect plenty of lively debate before the Park comes into existence in 2008.

the island and home to the MacEwen family that has owned Muck since 1895. With sandy beaches and views across to Rum on clear days, it is a fine spot to while away time.

Muck's southern coast is more rugged with the cliffs at An Leachdach holding good numbers of breeding seabirds in summer: look for kittiwake, guillemot and razorbill on the ledges and shags on the boulders below. Puffins also once nested on Muck, but the presence of brown rats has seen them move to offshore sanctuaries

such as Horse Island, which can be reached on foot during a low spring tide.

Many visitors also make the short hike to the summit of Ben Aerean, the island's highest point at just 150m. From here, there are wonderful views down on to Camas Mòr – a fine example of Jurassic limestone pavement – and across the wider island chain.

For more information, including a walking map, be sure to drop in to the excellent craft shop in Port Mor when open in the summer months.

Harbour porpoises surface quickly and show little of their bodies

A hauntingly beautiful chain of around 200 islands, the Western Isles extend for more than 200km along the edge of northwest Europe. With very little between here and Canada, the western coasts are constantly battered by the Atlantic. It is an erosive action that, combined with an ever present wind, has created miles of white sand beaches and dunes.

However, it is the narrow strip of fertile machair grassland behind the dunes that contributes most to the islands' abundance of life, including a renowned assemblage of wading birds. Further inland, the sandy grassland gives way to a peaty moorland studded with freshwater lochans – an altogether more hostile environment, but nonetheless home to plenty of specialist wildlife.

Journeying north from Barra to Lewis, through the heartland of Gaelic culture, this section explores all of these key habitats, as well as an offshore adventure around Uig in search of marine life.

The Western Isles are also a jumping-off point for several even more remote destinations, many of which are among Europe's most important seabird stations. With over a million seabirds, St Kilda is the most breathtaking of all, although there are numerous other islands to set the pulse racing.

Western Isles and beyond

Barra

Getting there **By ferry from Oban. Flights from Glasgow** OS Map **Landranger 31**

Colourful and compact, easy-going Barra offers a fine introduction to the fragile coastal habitat of the Western Isles.

Cut adrift at the southern end of the Western Isles, Barra provides a delicious snapshot of the natural beauty typical of this striking archipelago. The island's rugged interior is fringed by white sand beaches, sweeping machair and numerous rocky coves that invite further exploration.

Barra is also an island of two distinct coastlines: while the east is largely sheltered and rocky, the west coast feels the full force of the fearsome Atlantic surf – a constant reminder of just how exposed this island chain is.

Most visitors arrive by ferry at Castlebay from where a circular road travels around the island. To the south, a causeway links Barra with Vatersay, the most southerly inhabited island in the Western Isles. In spring and summer, the machair on the narrow isthmus that separates Bagh Siar from Vatersay Bay is carpeted in wildflowers and is a good area to hear (and maybe see) the secretive corncrake.

Vatersay Bay itself can be a good spot for otters, while razorbill and other seabirds from the colonies at Mingulay and Berneray fish in the clear waters – their silvery outlines visible as they zip underwater in pursuit of prey.

Back on Barra, the north of the island is dominated by Traigh Mhor (or Cockle Strand), an expanse of sand that, at low tide,

Oystercatchers are a familiar sight across the Western Isles

serves as the runway for Barra's airport. Landing on a beach of clean white sand while islanders hand rake for cockles nearby is one of the world's more unusual aviation experiences.

A variety of shorebirds also make full use of the rich pickings, including the distinctive – and noisy – oystercatcher. Easily recognised with its red eyes and orange bill, the birds frantically probe the sand for cockles, often with a steady accompaniment of high-pitched kleeps.

Further north still, the croft land around St Barr's Church (Cille Bharra) at Eoligarry is among the best on the island for corncrake, with several males calling regularly from the deep cover each season. It is also a wonderfully colourful area in summer, with wave upon wave of wildflowers sweeping down to the shore.

Nearby, the pristine beach that heads from the old jetty at Eoligarry to Scurrival Point provides fine views to the tiny island of Fiaray: look for bobbing seals and gannets plunge diving further out in the sound. Basking shark and common dolphin are often seen from the shore, as well as from the ferry that crosses from Ardmhor to Friskay.

For a more hands-on experience of Barra's marine life, Clearwater Paddling based at Dunard Lodge in Castlebay offers a range of sea kayaking trips that are ideal for beginners.

Outer islands

To the south of Barra lie three uninhabited islands – Pabbay, Mingulay and Berneray – whose history, isolation and bird life draw comparisons with those of far away St Kilda. Now in the care of the National Trust for Scotland, the islands have been deserted since 1912 when the last inhabitants gave in to the elements. Today, Mingulay and Berneray are known for the seabirds that nest on the islands' towering west cliffs. This includes Scotland's largest colony of razorbills (17,000 pairs), as well as fulmar, guillemot and puffin along the clifftops. Ask at the tourist information centre in Castlebay for details on boat trips to the islands.

◀ Machair at Eoligarry

Loch Druidibeg, South Uist Scottish Natural Heritage

Getting there Either side of A865 in
central South Uist near Stilligarry
OS Map Landranger 22

**Famed for its breeding waders, greylag
geese and raptors, Loch Druidibeg offers
a varied slice of South Uist life.**

Stretching inland from the Atlantic almost
as far as the Minch, Loch Druidibeg
National Nature Reserve exhibits a clear
progression in habitat from fertile coastal
grassland to acidic peat moorland – with a
corresponding range of wildlife.

At its Atlantic edge, the reserve is
dominated by the dramatic beach and dune
system that stretches in an almost
unbroken line along the western margins of
the Uists and Benbecula. Behind the dunes,
the flower-rich machair provides a mosaic
of habitats that attracts one of the highest
densities of breeding waders in Europe.

Each species occupies a slightly different
niche: oystercatcher and ringed plover nest
on the beach itself or the ploughed land,
lapwing prefer the drier pasture behind the

dunes and dunlin the damp machair, while
redshank and snipe use wetter areas.

Crofters also make wide use of the coastal
grasslands, contributing to the biodiversity
by growing low-intensity fodder crops and
grazing livestock in winter. The use of storm
tossed seaweed as an organic fertiliser only
adds to the plenty.

Further inland, between the machair and
the moor, the loch and surrounding wetlands
provide a wintering and breeding ground for
a small colony of wild greylag geese – part
of a wider population of around 5,000 birds
spread throughout the Uists and Benbecula.

At its western margins, Loch Druidibeg
itself is enriched by wind-blown sand and is
relatively fertile. Further east, however, it is
much less productive as the terrain turns to
bog and heather moorland. Dominated by the
summit of nearby Hecla (606m), this is prime
upland habitat: buzzard, hen harrier and
short-eared owl hunt over the reserve, while
a handful of red deer roam the lower slopes.

Although the surrounding landscape is
bleak, the many islands that dot Loch

◄ Remote moorland above Loch Druidibeg

Hedgehog cull

Although still present in large numbers, many of Uist's wader species have experienced massive decline – with the blame placed squarely on egg predation by hedgehogs. The animals, introduced to South Uist in the 1970s, emerge from hibernation just as the birds begin nesting and happily supplement their mainly invertebrate diet with the nutritious eggs. The threat to the wader population is such that, in 2003, SNH began a programme of 'wader recovery' with the ultimate goal of removing hedgehogs from the Uists and Benbecula altogether.

Druidibeg hold a cover of wind-battered scrub – remnants of native woodland that have maintained a toehold away from grazing animals.

A large reserve, Loch Druidibeg is best explored along a circular trail (8km) that starts from a parking area on the B890 and heads west through boggy moorland and onto the machair (trail guides available from outside the SNH office just south of

Stilligarry). Look out for golden eagle circling overhead and, in summer, golden plover calling from the tops of heather mounds.

Elsewhere, the beach can also be reached via the historic crofting settlement of Howmore. This is a wonderful place to sit amongst the dunes and watch the sun go down – and maybe even spot an otter foraging along the shoreline.

Golden plover occupy breeding grounds from May to September

Balranald, North Uist RSPB Reserve

Getting there **Northwest coast of North Uist, turn off A865 to Hougharry. Visitor centre (open year round)** OS Map **Landranger 18**

Sparkling machair, abundant bird life and tantalising views of distant islands all contribute to Balranald's special charm.

A colourful contrast to the patchwork of peaty lochans that cover much of North Uist, the northwest coast contains some of the finest machair habitat anywhere in the Uists. This is no more so than at Balranald, an RSPB reserve that juts out into the Atlantic near the crofting township of Hougharry.

Shaped by the low-intensity farming practiced by generations of crofters,

Balranald has a particularly diverse machair that holds more than 50 species of breeding birds in the summer.

Inland, a scattering of freshwater pools provides plentiful cover for wildfowl and other animals: tufted duck and – unusually for the Western Isles – several pairs of shoveler regularly breed amongst the reed beds, while otters also hunt around the pools.

The reserve is at its most lively between April and July when the wet grassland is alive with the sound of hundreds of waders. Lapwing, redshank and oystercatcher are plentiful, while there are smaller numbers of dunlin and snipe. Fortunately, the hedgehogs that have wreaked such havoc in Benbecula and South Uist have yet to make it this far north.

Ringed plover at the nest

But Balranald is perhaps best known for its corncrake population, with more than 30 calling males on the reserve each season. And this is one place where these pathologically shy birds can actually be seen as well as heard: a few brazen males have taken to calling in full view around the visitor centre. May to June is often the best time to see them.

The reserve can be explored along a circular trail (4.5km) that leads from the visitor centre to the rocky headland at Aird an Runair and back along the coast. On a clear day, the views stretch as far as distant St Kilda.

In summer, a variety of whales and dolphins – including orcas – feed close inshore, but the low vantage point and, often, choppy conditions make them tough to spot. Much more readily seen are the plentiful grey seals from the colony on the nearby Monach Isles that regularly haul out around the coast.

Further north, the trail skirts an area used by nesting Arctic terns, a species that will make it known if anyone has stepped too close. Tread carefully, too, if walking along the beach: ringed plover nest on the shingle and the birds' well-camouflaged eggs are easily trampled.

From May to late-August, RSPB rangers run two regular guided walks: a tour of the Balranald machair (Tues mornings) and an otter walk that starts at Langais Hotel (Wed mornings). Check at the visitor centre for details.

The Monach Isles

Some 12km west of North Uist, the Monach Isles (or Heisker) are clearly visible from Balranald. Managed as a National Nature Reserve by SNH, these five low-lying machair islands are home to the largest colony of grey seals in the UK (and the world's second largest after Sable Island, Nova Scotia). Numbers peak in October when up to 8,000 pups are born on the beaches. The islands also hold Scotland's highest density of black guillemots, with around 800 individuals. Poor weather can make the Monachs tricky to reach, but local charters are available: ask at the Uist Outdoor Centre or the nearby tourist information centre in Lochmaddy.

◄ Traigh Iar, Balranald

North Harris Hills

Getting there Parking at Huishinish Bay
at end of B887, North Harris
OS Map Landranger 13

**A potentially strenuous walk that
highlights some of the wildlife found
as the mountains meet the sea in
North Harris.**

The winding road that travels beneath the
North Harris hills on its way to Huishinish
snakes through a supremely elemental
landscape; rock and water are the dominant
features until the views are softened by
another Harris speciality – a pristine white
sand beach at Huishinish Bay.

A fine spot for a swim, Huishinish Bay is
also the start point for a 3km trek (one way)
to Cravadale. It is an area where habitats
collide: those with keen eyes, and a little
luck, are as likely to spot a golden eagle
soaring above the cliffs as dolphins
swimming in the clear waters below.

From the car park opposite the bay,
continue towards Huishinish for 200m
before heading north along a sandy track
to reach the coast just east of a small
jetty. From here, the old Cravadale path
passes through two gates before rising,
steeply in places, to traverse the side of
Husival Beag.

As the path gains height, there are
fabulous views across the sound to Scarp.
Once home to more than 200 people, the
island is now deserted and strong winds
have taken their toll on the abandoned
dwellings.

Treacherous currents in the sound often
prevented Scarp's inhabitants from reaching

Fringe benefits

The subject of a thousand postcards, Highland cattle are found all over Scotland, but are perhaps most in their element in the harsh conditions of the Western Isles. The animals' photogenic looks belie a hardy character: literally impervious to wind and rain thanks to a double-layered coat, Highlanders prosper in areas of poor grazing and have long made a vital economic contribution in many upland areas. The animals' distinctive fringe (or dossan) protects the eyes from the elements in winter and keeps flies at bay during the summer.

Harris and communication between the two islands was difficult at best. This led to a famous experiment in 1934 when a German scientist attempted to deliver mail between the two islands by rocket. Sadly, the concept of 'rocket post' proved short lived: the projectile exploded on its first flight, showering the beach with scorched letters.

As the path passes beneath steep buttresses, keep an eye out not just for golden eagle, but also buzzard and raven – the latter often making its presence heard before it is seen. Look out, too, for seabirds on the cliffs below the path.

After 1km, the path climbs gradually inland to a saddle at Gresclett before dropping down to the boggy shores of Loch na Cleavag. The loch can be skirted in either direction, although a good – if damp – option is to skirt the eastern shore passing a lone cottage to reach the head of Loch Cravadale.

If height is the goal, Husival Beag (306m) can be tackled along its northern corrie, otherwise continue beyond the slight rise of Meilein and return along the white sands of Traigh Mheilein to eventually rejoin the path.

Take your time, however: Loch Cravadale is good otter country, while the temptation to sit quietly and enjoy the splendid isolation of Traigh Mheilein can be hard to resist.

◀ Scarp from Traigh Mheilein

St Kilda National Trust for Scotland

Getting there **65km west of North Uist. Day trips from Harris (Kilda Cruises), plus cruise ships/charters from Oban, Lewis and North Uist** OS Map **Landranger 18**

Far-flung and breathtakingly wild, St Kilda is one of Scotland's most outstanding natural spectacles.

The most remote community in Britain until the last islanders were evacuated in 1930, St Kilda is a dual World Heritage Site, listed both for its natural environment and cultural significance. It is also an iconic destination for adventurous travellers, with the sheer difficulty of access only adding to its mystique.

Bequeathed to the National Trust for Scotland in 1957, St Kilda is managed as a National Nature Reserve. Regular volunteer groups, coordinated by a summer warden, undertake conservation and survey work around the old village on the main island of Hirta, plus long-term monitoring of the wildlife and archaeology around the archipelago.

The only year-round inhabitants are the civilian contractors employed by the MoD to operate a radar tracking station for its missile range on Benbecula.

From a wildlife perspective, St Kilda is best known as Europe's premier seabird station: more than a million birds nest here each season. It is a wildlife extravaganza that includes the UK's largest colonies of fulmar and puffin, while the outlying island of Boreray and neighbouring sea stacks – Stac Lee and the fang-like Stac an Armin – hold the world's largest colony of gannets (around 60,000 pairs).

Up close, it is difficult to know what is more impressive: the seething mass of life, or the savage grandeur of the towering cliffs on which the birds nest.

Until recently, the only way to reach

◀ One of the many cleits high on Hirta

Seabirds for supper

Fowling was a way of life for St Kildans, with the seabirds that nest around the islands a vital source of food and income. The islanders braved dangerous swells and treacherous cliffs to harvest gannets, puffins and fulmars on Boreray and elsewhere. In 1876, they were said to have harvested nearly 89,000 puffins alone. Eggs provided valuable nourishment in summer, while little was wasted of the birds themselves: the carcasses were plucked, dried and stored in cleits for the winter, while the oil and feathers were kept for export or to pay rent.

St Kilda was on live aboard cruise vessels, but day trips are now available from Harris with Kilda Cruises (April to Sept). It takes 2.5 hours to reach the islands, with up to five hours spent on Hirta. The weather, however, is a major factor: book early and be prepared for schedule changes and rough seas.

Landing parties on Hirta receive a brief orientation from the warden before setting off to explore. The single 'street' of the village itself is hugely poignant with a line of ruined blackhouses interspersed with partly restored cottages, while the slopes above are dotted with hundreds of cleits – stone storehouses used by islanders to keep provisions cool and dry.

Primitive Soay sheep roam wild around the village, while St Kilda's very own subspecies of wren and field mouse are sometimes seen amongst the ruins.

Elsewhere, the high ground above the village at Mullach Mor is reached via the MoD road, with many visitors also making the final push to Conachair (376m), the highest sea cliff in Britain. Needless to say, the views are extraordinary, but beware: the high moorland is inhabited by a lively colony of great skuas that dive-bomb anyone who strays too close to a nest.

Up close, gannets are surprisingly colourful birds

53

Uig coast, Lewis

Getting there **West coast of Lewis, off B8011. RIB trips available from Miavaig (Seatrek)** OS Map **Landranger 13**

Blessed with the finest coastline on Lewis, Uig's dramatic landscape is best appreciated from the water.

It is quite a drive to the remote parish of Uig, but travellers are rewarded with the most scenic landscape anywhere on Lewis. The craggy interior and complex coastline, full of narrow inlets, secret coves and glorious beaches, make for an alluring combination.

An outdoor playground, Uig comes into its own in July during the annual Hebridean Challenge. A multi-discipline adventure race, the 'Heb' sees participants run, mountain bike, swim and kayak along the length of the Western Isles, covering a course up to 700km in length. The Uig hills and inshore waters are often used for hill running and sea kayak sections.

Participants may not have the time – or energy – to appreciate it, but Uig's fractured coastline holds many geological and natural treasures. All around, there is ample evidence of the astonishing power of the winter storms that assault this exposed area of coast. From Bernera to the end of the road at Mealasta, the surging Atlantic has battered the cliffs into a series of stacks and arches, while many of the headlands have been stripped bare of vegetation by the crashing waves.

Wildlife flourishes despite the harsh conditions, although the widespread presence of non-native mink poses a real

Uig's waters hold a
variety of marine life

threat to many coastal species. Colonial ground nesting birds are at particular risk from this versatile predator, while even the red-throated divers that nest on hillside lochans can be vulnerable.

Such is the danger to native wildlife that the Hebridean Mink Project – a partnership between SNH, the RSPB and other conservation bodies – has spent considerable time and money removing the animals from South Harris and the Uists. The project's trappers now plan to take on the much greater challenge of eradicating mink from Lewis and the remainder of Harris.

Uig's most impressive wildlife, however, is found offshore, where year round residents such as grey seals and common dolphins are joined in summer by basking sharks, minke whales and even the occasional pod of orcas (killer whales) that ply the waters between here and Shetland.

Although sometimes seen from headlands, Uig's marine life is best enjoyed from the water. Sea kayakers will enjoy the clear waters and sheltered islands in and around Loch Roag, while visitors can cover more ground – and at considerably higher speed – with Seatrek, a long-established RIB operator that provides wildlife trips around inshore waters from the jetty at Miavaig (May to Sept).

Peatlands in peril

At first glance, a proposal by British Energy to construct a windfarm on the North Lewis peatlands seems a good plan: there is plenty of wind to harness, while the development would bring jobs to local communities and contribute to Scotland's wider renewable energy targets. However, the sheer scale of the project – with more than 200 turbines stretching for 30km – and its location on a fragile habitat that supports many of Scotland's most precious breeding species has met with determined opposition from local residents and conservation bodies. The final decision rests with the Scottish Executive, although such is the strength of feeling that a lengthy delay is likely.

◀ Sea kayakers off Reef Beach

Tiumpan Head, Lewis

Getting there On northeast tip of the Eye Peninsula, off A866 OS Map Landranger 8

With panoramic views over the Minch, Tiumpan Head is an ideal vantage point for spotting whales and dolphins passing close inshore.

The most northeasterly point on Lewis's protruding Eye Peninsula, Tiumpan Head is a famous headland with elevated views across the Minch and Broad Bay. Once an important defensive position ideal for spying the approach of enemy vessels, it is now used for spotting a very different kind of marine activity: whales and dolphins.

Traditionally, Hebridean waters enjoy high levels of cetacean (whale, dolphin and porpoise) activity thanks in part to the stirring up of food supplies by the strong tidal streams and complex underwater topography around the islands.

Tiumpan Head itself is one of several points used as an onshore look-out point during the Sea Watch Foundation's annual census of cetacean activity in British waters. And while there are no guarantees, there is plenty to look out for: Risso's dolphins are frequent visitors to Broad Bay, white-beaked dolphins have been seen from the headland in late summer and sightings of common dolphins have increased in many Hebridean waters.

Minke whale surfacing

Focus on minkes

The cold water-loving minke whale has been the focus of a long-running study by the Mull-based Hebridean Whale and Dolphin Trust, which has identified more than 75 individuals that inhabit Hebridean waters during the summer. Animals are photographed and catalogued according to distinctive features such as fin marks and body scars. It is a process sometimes aided by the animal's natural inquisitiveness and inclination to approach research and tour boats. The position of feeding minkes is often given away by gatherings of noisy seabirds on and around the water — something to look out for when whale watching from Tiumpan Head

During the often split second sightings, it is difficult to identify one species from another, although the large Risso's dolphins (up to 4m in length) can generally be identified by a rounded head and pencil like markings on its flanks. White-beaked dolphins, a smaller (up to 3m) and more active species when at the surface, have stumpy white beaks, while the common dolphin (up to 2.4m) has a long beak and a yellow-tinged pattern on its side.

Between May and October, minke whales also pass close inshore in the deep waters surrounding the headland. Sleek and with a torpedo-like snout that breaks the water first, adults grow to between seven and 10 metres in length.

Usually solitary, minkes can sometimes be seen in pairs around feeding grounds. The smallest of the world's baleen whales, minkes feed by filtering food through baleen plates that hang down from their top jaws. The plates effectively act like a giant sieve, trapping prey such as herring and sandeels as the whale takes in huge volumes of seawater. Many of the animals that frequent Scottish waters in summer are believed to return to the same areas to feed year after year.

Budding whale watchers can park by the now automated lighthouse at Tiumpan Head and explore around much of the headland — with spectacular views across the Minch to the Assynt hills and south to Skye. And if the seas are quiet, there is always the small but busy seabird colony north of the lighthouse to enjoy.

◄ Tiumpan Head lighthouse

The Shiants and other outlying islands

Getting there **Shiant Islands** (7km east of Lewis); **Flannan Isles** (32km west of Lewis); **Rona and Sula Sgeir** (70km north of Butt of Lewis) OS Map **Landranger 8, 13 and 14**

Destinations for serious mariners, the many outlying islands of the Western Isles offer wildlife and adventure in equal measure.

While the Western Isles can reasonably be considered remote in their own right, they provide a springboard for several islands that take isolation to another level. None are straightforward to reach, but with the right planning and a sufficient window of fine weather, all provide a memorable experience.

Closest to hand are the Shiants, a trio of islands that loom out of the Minch some 8km southeast of Lewis. Geologically rich,

with sheer cliffs of columnar basalt, the islands are also a major seabird station with around 250,000 individuals, including a vast number of puffins.

Interestingly, the seabird population appears stable despite the presence of black rats – normally a threat to seabird colonies. Dropping analysis by SNH suggests that the rats might be feeding mainly on vegetative matter, although more work is needed to determine accurate levels of egg predation.

Different again are the Flannan Isles, a group of seven low-lying islands some 32km west of Lewis. The islands, also known as the Seven Hunters, are famous for the unexplained disappearance of three lighthouse keepers in December 1900.

Again, seabirds rule the roost, with particularly large numbers of puffin, plus a

Fulmars nest on many of the islands

strong gannet colony. Landing can be dicey, but in the right conditions it is possible to explore the main island of Eilean Mor with its now automated lighthouse.

More remote still are Rona and Sula Sgeir, two tiny islands 70km north of Lewis and managed as a National Nature Reserve (by SNH). Rona is home to 15 species of breeding seabird, including the rare Leach's petrel – a tiny nocturnal seabird that calls from nest burrows in the ruins of an old village. Rona also holds a well-studied grey seal colony, with up to 1000 pups born each autumn.

Sula Sgeir, meanwhile, is the last place in Britain where gannets are still harvested for human consumption. Every August, following a centuries-old tradition, hunters depart from Port of Ness on Lewis to share gugas (gannet chicks).

Although gannets are a protected species, the Ness men have a special dispensation from the Scottish Executive that allows them to catch up to 2000 gugas each season. The birds are plucked, singed and salted, before being boiled and served with potatoes. The meat is said to be strong in flavour and extremely fishy.

A variety of operators offer trips – try Seatrek (Lewis), Island Cruising (Lewis) and Guideliner Hebridean (Skye) – although there is no formal set up for any of the islands. The situation can change from year to year and it is best to check local tourist information centres. SNH requests that visitors to Rona or Sula Sgeir make contact first, preferably at its Stornoway office.

Make room for Sea Room

The cultural history, wildlife and geology of the Shiant Islands are lovingly told by their owner, Adam Nicolson, in his 2000 book, *Sea Room*. It is an evocative insight not just into the Shiants, but also the wider way of life in this part of the Hebrides. Visitors wishing to stay on the islands can make use of a basic house on Eilean an Tighe (House Island), but should contact the owner first to ensure that visits do not conflict with the work of the grazing tenant.

◄ The Shiants from Pairc

A chain of more than 70 islands, Orkney lies across the Pentland Firth just 10km from the Scottish mainland. Orcadian first, Scottish second and with a distinctly Scandinavian twist, the islanders are justly proud of their wildlife and rich archaeological history.

Orkney is particularly renowned for the diversity of its bird life and it is no coincidence that the RSPB is a major landowner. However, with species as charismatic as they are accessible, Orkney is a destination for all lovers of wild places and not just the serious birdwatcher.

This chapter opens with three sites – and distinct habitats – on Mainland Orkney before exploring five outlying islands. First stop is rugged Hoy with its no-nonsense bonxies and Old Man, before heading to the central island of Eday to enjoy its unusually high density of red-throated divers.

Further north still are three islands where the pounding Atlantic exerts a particularly strong influence: the cliffs and maritime heath on Westray and Papa Westray offer an absorbing seabird experience, while Sanday's kelp forests provide food and shelter for a huge variety of life – including an abundance of common seals.

All are bewitching destinations easily enjoyed during the long, lazy days of an Orcadian summer.

Orkney

Marwick Head RSPB Reserve

Getting there **17km** north of Stromness.
Access from Marwick Bay or Cumlaquoy
(both off B9056) OS Map **Landranger 6**

**One of Orkney's top seabird sites,
Marwick Head offers fine clifftop walks
amidst the clamour of 50,000 seabirds.**

Orkney's underlying old red sandstone is
shown off to great effect at Marwick Head
where the 1.6km-long cliffs have weathered
perfectly to provide a multi-storey summer
home to one of Orkney's top gatherings of
breeding seabirds. With salt-loving
flowering plants colouring the clifftops and
the crashing ocean far below, it can be a
wonderful place in which to linger.

In a good season, these 85m-high cliffs
hold up to 25,000 tightly packed
guillemots, although the many ledges also
support several thousand pairs of kittiwake
and smaller numbers of fulmar. Elsewhere,
razorbill nest close to the cliff edge in
places, while the keen-eyed may even spot
the small number of puffins that also breed
along the cliffs. Take care, however: a good
head for heights is needed at some of the
more precarious viewpoints.

Inevitably, such a large gathering of
seabirds attracts predators: peregrine falcon
sometimes hunt along the cliffs, with rock
doves a particular favourite, while great and
Arctic skuas can be seen chasing smaller
seabirds to steal their catch and even
taking chicks.

Presiding over the highest part of the
cliffs is the Kitchener memorial, a tower

Nesting shag

Seabirds and settlements

An uninhabited islet north of Marwick Head, the Brough of Birsay is reached via a narrow concrete causeway accessible for around two hours either side of low tide. The Brough has its own seabird cliffs, plus the remains of a large settlement that was an important seat of power first for Pictish and then Norse settlers. The heavily indented coastline around the lighthouse provides fine views of seabirds at the nest – including a handful of green-plumaged shags. The birds' dishevelled nests indicate a certain resourcefulness, with sticks, seaweed, discarded rope and other items used in their construction.

erected in the memory of Lord Kitchener, the Secretary of State for War and one of more than 650 men to perish during the sinking of *HMS Hampshire* off Marwick Head in June 1916. Hugely influential at the time, Kitchener is best known today as the moustachioed figure on the famous 'Your country needs you' recruitment posters.

The most direct approach to Marwick Head is from the small car park at Cumlaqouy, although the path that winds up from Marwick Bay a kilometre or so further south offers a much more scenic option. Starting from beside the Choin – a tidal lagoon that attracts many waders, ducks and geese – the path gradually gains height to slowly reveal more of the cliffs.

On a clear day, there are fine views to the lighthouse on the Brough of Birsay some 4km further north, while the sight, sound and smell of the seabirds fills the senses. In summer, a pair of ravens usually nests beneath the monument, adding their throaty croaks and aerial acrobatics to the overall spectacle.

Not surprisingly given its elevation and westerly aspect, Marwick Head is a prime spot to savour Orkney's often spectacular sunsets. Silhouetted seabirds and the warm red glow of the cliffs as the sun dips into the Atlantic can make for a perfect end to what is a long summer's day this far north.

◄ Marwick Head and the distant Brough of Birsay

The Loons RSPB Reserve

Getting there **Access via unmarked minor road 1.6km east of Marwick Head**
OS Map Landranger 6

One of Orkney's finest wetland areas, The Loons and nearby Loch of Banks hold an extraordinary variety of life throughout the year.

A visit to The Loons early on a spring morning shows off this wetland reserve at its very best: the air is full of the frantic calls of displaying waders with lapwing, redshank, curlew and snipe all contributing to what is a rousing start to the day.

Now a relatively scarce habitat in Orkney, with many similar areas drained for agricultural use, the basin mire complex at The Loons includes a mix of wet grassland, marsh and open water. The area has a long history as a cattle-grazing marsh – a land use that continues today – while peat was also once cut here.

Although the word 'loon' is another term for the diver group of birds, none are thought to have ever bred here. Instead, the name comes from an Old Norse word 'lon' which means an expanse of meadow beside open water.

The sheer variety of habitat found in such a relatively small area attracts not just a rich assemblage of waders, but also a large colony of black-headed gulls and more than 10 species of breeding duck. Shoveler, wigeon and teal are all present in high numbers, while avid birdwatchers have a treat in store: the reserve holds around half a dozen of the 40 or so pairs of pintail that breed in the UK.

But the beauty of this site is that visitors can never quite be sure what will turn up.

◀ Open water in front of the reserve hide

In spring and summer, short-eared owl and hen harrier hunt Orkney vole over drier parts of the reserve, while kittiwakes from nearby Marwick Head collect wet grass for use in nest building early in the season.

Although much quieter in winter, the reserve nonetheless remains important.

Sound of spring

With its head crest and predominantly black and white plumage lifted by a green and purple sheen, the lapwing is the most distinctive of all the waders found at The Loons. Although the birds feed during the day, picking off insects and earthworms at the surface of the soil, they do so much more vigorously at night – a tactic employed partly to avoid food being stolen by black-headed gulls. The birds are most conspicuous, however, during their spring display flights when the male zigzags through the sky in a series of vocal rolls and tumbles.

Large numbers of wildfowl winter in Orkney with the wigeon that arrive from Iceland each autumn particularly numerous. More rare is the flock of 100-plus Greenland white-fronted geese that arrive in late-September, while whooper swans and greylag geese also overwinter at The Loons and in surrounding fields.

Good views across the wet meadows can be enjoyed year round from a raised viewpoint west of Spurdagrove, plus a large hide nearby. Meanwhile, Loch of Banks – considered part of the reserve despite being 2km away – can be viewed from the main road (A986) north of Dounby.

Birsay Moors RSPB Reserve

Getting there **Bordered by Loch of Swannay (north), Mid Tooin (south), Burgar Hill (east) and Durkadale (west). Access via B9057** OS Map **Landranger 6**

Hen harrier and short-eared owl are just two of the striking species that breed on the rolling Birsay Moors.

Dark, brooding and seemingly lifeless in winter, the moorland, marsh and bog that blankets the RSPB's sprawling Birsay Moors reserve comes alive in spring with a remarkable assemblage of breeding species.

Orkney has the highest density of curlew in the UK and several thousand nest on the lower moorland, their bubbling calls signalling the arrival of spring. They are joined in wetter areas by snipe, while oystercatchers appear at almost every turn.

And there is just as much activity on higher ground with skuas, dunlin and golden plover all present. Nearby, red-throated divers nest on remote hill lochans,

although they are best seen from the hide that overlooks Lowrie's Water beneath the wind turbines at Burgar Hill. The hide is accessed from a minor road just outside Evie: aim for the middle turbine and follow the RSPB signs.

The high moorland around Burgar Hill is also home to Orkney's famed population of raptors. Hardest to spot is the fast-moving merlin, a small falcon that feeds mainly on songbirds. More obvious are the kestrels that hover above the moor and short-eared owls that perch on roadside fenceposts, their yellow eyes blazing. A daytime hunter, the owls are often seen quartering the ground on moth-like wings.

However, of all its raptors, Orkney is best known for its hen harriers. With no managed grouse moors on Orkney, the birds have traditionally prospered here without the persecution seen on mainland Scotland. Their profile was also raised considerably by the Orcadian ornithologist, Eddie Balfour,

Hen harrier on the nest

Sky dancing

There are few more impressive springtime sights than the 'sky dancing' display of the hen harrier – an aerial courtship (best seen in early April) in which the male flies in an elaborate series of dives and swoops. The smaller, grey coloured male is polygamous and attempts to provide for several females each season. However, the more females he has in tow, the less able he is to provide sufficient food for all of the chicks. When food is brought to the nest, the female rises up out of the heather for a spectacular mid-air food pass before returning to her brood.

whose 30-year study of the species began at nearby Cottascarth in the 1940s.

Sadly, low breeding productivity has seen numbers decline markedly since Balfour's day, although Birsay Moors still support around 15 territories. It is a decline blamed largely on the loss of suitable habitat for the Orkney vole, a sub-species unique to Orkney and the hen harrier's chief item of prey.

The RSPB has responded by trialling muirburning and livestock grazing to create a more suitable mosaic of heather and rough grassland for the voles, while SNH has introduced a management scheme to encourage farmers to develop vole-friendly wildlife corridors in areas adjacent to moorland.

Birsay Moors is best explored along the Evie to Dounby road (B9057) and the adjoining Hillside road that runs through Durkadale to the east of Greeny Hill. There are parking areas, a layby at Howally and plenty of old peat cutters' tracks to investigate. In winter, there is also a substantial hen harrier roost – with up to 25 birds – on the southeast slopes of Greeny Hill.

◀ Birsay's open moorland

North Hoy RSPB Reserve

Getting there **By ferry from Stromness to Moaness (passenger only) and Houton to Lyness (cars)** OS Map **Landranger 7**

With wildlife as uncompromising as its landscape, Hoy offers a very different kind of Orkney experience.

Most visitors' first glimpse of Hoy – and its famous Old Man – is from the ferry that runs from the Scottish mainland to Stromness. It is a tantalising taste of a rugged island that stands out in what is a largely fertile, low-lying archipelago.

Much of Hoy is sparsely populated, with the heather-clad hill ground in the northwest a particularly unforgiving environment. But it is in this large area, much of it managed by the RSPB as a nature reserve, that Hoy's diversity of moorland life can best be enjoyed.

The absence of Orkney vole means that hen harrier and short-eared owl are relatively thin on the ground, but merlin, kestrel and buzzard are all present, while a variety of breeding waders join a small population of red grouse amongst the heather.

Hoy is, however, best known for holding up to 20 per cent of the world's breeding population of great skuas (or bonxies). Around 2000 pairs of these combative birds nest each summer (April-July) together with 200 pairs of the smaller but no less aggressive Arctic skua.

Much of the island's wildlife can be experienced on the way to the Old Man of Hoy, a celebrated landmark that draws a steady stream of visitors through the beautifully located crofting settlement at Rackwick.

For those with a car, the single-track road to Rackwick is one of Orkney's finest drives,

Climbing tackle the Old Man

Climbing the Old Man

Although first conquered in a famous televised climb led by Chris Bonington in 1966, the 137m high Old Man of Hoy remains a considerable challenge for experienced climbers to this day. With just seabirds for company and the roaring waves far below, it must make for a dramatic ascent. No one is quite sure, however, just how long the Old Man will be around to pose its unique challenge: the layers of sandstone are showing signs of severe erosion, while the plug of hard volcanic basalt that protects the Old Man's base will not resist the battering of winter storms forever.

although the walk in via a 3.5-km trail from Sandy Loch is equally impressive. Sandy Loch itself is a favourite bathing spot for red-throated divers, while the first of Hoy's bonxies are often seen in the area.

Heath spotted orchid, sundew and butterwort all flourish in boggy areas, while the trail also passes Berriedale Wood, an atmospheric gully that shelters the UK's most northerly native woodland.

From Rackwick Bay, it is a further 4km to the Old Man. The boulder fields along the way are home to mountain hare, while the cliffs around the Old Man teem with a variety of seabirds, including good numbers of fulmar and puffin – although the latter can be difficult to spot. In fine weather, it is also worth continuing to crumbling St

John's Head, one of the UK's highest sea cliffs (378m).

All around, however, there is no ignoring the bonxies that stand guard over nest sites that are little more than scrapes in the ground. Bonxies defend their territories with vigour and it is best to stick to the path – particularly around the Stourdale plateau where walkers risk receiving additional attention from a large colony of great black-backed gulls.

Arctic Skua calling

◄ Rackwick Bay in mist.

Eday

Getting there **Ferries and flights from Kirkwall, Mainland** OS Map **Landranger 5**

Although home to many classic Orkney species, Eday is best known for its high density of breeding red-throated divers.

With its heather-clad upland interior, many of Eday's 120 or so residents are scattered along a strip of fertile coastal land – although the numerous derelict buildings suggest Eday was once home to a much larger population.

From a wildlife perspective, the north of the island has the greatest interest. Travelling from the ferry berth at Backaland in the south, visitors pass through a peaty landscape that holds more life than first meets the eye: short-eared owl, curlew and skuas are all present, while Flaughton Hill has a handful of breeding whimbrel – a smaller cousin of the curlew and a rarity in Orkney.

The principal wildlife attraction, however, is found at Mill Loch, a body of freshwater that supports up to a dozen pairs of breeding red-throated diver – an unusually high number for a single loch. This elegant Arctic species has its UK stronghold in Shetland, although Orkney also holds a healthy population.

Red-throated divers are unusual amongst seabirds in that they nest on small inland lochans, but feed at sea. With bills slightly raised and red throats clearly visible in summer, the birds are a picture of poise on the water, but desperately clumsy on land.

A hide overlooking the loch provides great views of the divers (April-Sept) on the water and as they depart for fishing trips. With a high wing loading, divers are not the most agile of flyers and often make several circuits of the loch as they gradually gain lift.

The hide also marks the start of the Eday

◀ The Stone of Setter

Heritage Trail, a 6km loop that includes many of the island's most interesting archaeological sites. Chief among them is the nearby Stone of Setter, although the chambered cairns on Vinquoy Hill are also impressive.

Red Head, the highest point on the trail, offers fine views across much of Orkney and the nearby Calf of Eday. Uninhabited since the early Iron Age, the island's collection of chambered tombs and prehistoric dwellings makes it one of the most important sites of its kind in the UK.

The lack of disturbance has also allowed wildlife to flourish: there is a large cormorant colony in the south, colonies of great skuas (bonxies) and great black-backed gulls inland, plus nesting seabirds around Grey Head. Grey seals also often linger around the Graand on the west side of the island.

Boats operate to the Calf on demand in summer, while guided tours of Eday itself (including historic Carrick House) are also available. Ask on the ferry or at the tourist office in Kirkwall for details.

Red-throated diver with young

Rain geese

Red-throated divers are known as rain geese in Orkney and Shetland where their mournful calls are said to foretell the coming of wet weather. With legs set well back on their bodies, the birds are built for swimming rather than walking. As a result, their basic nests are usually constructed close to the water's edge. The hide at Mill Loch provides a perfect way to enjoy a species that is extremely vulnerable to disturbance during the breeding season. Look out in particular for elaborate courtship displays that include pairs rearing up to clash chests and sudden parallel dashes across the water.

Sanday

Getting there **Ferries and flights from Kirkwall, Mainland** OS Map **Landranger 5**

Sanday's beaches are alluring, but it is the island's unseen forest of kelp that provides its lifeblood.

Sanday is well named, with the island's many bays containing a series of glorious sandy beaches. Impressive at any time, their true extent is revealed at low tide when vast expanses of sand flats provide feeding grounds for huge numbers of wading birds, particularly in winter.

In many parts of Sanday, the combination of exposed sand and plentiful wind has created a system of dunes and flower-rich machair more readily associated with Hebridean islands. Over the centuries, this wind-blown sand has covered the variety of archaeological sites for which the island is renowned; many have been excavated but plenty remain buried, their contours visible beneath the sandy grassland.

Although Sanday's beaches are its most conspicuous feature, it is the dense and largely unseen forest of kelp that fringes much of the coastline that gives the island its vitality. The kelp, sometimes spotted breaking the surface of the water at low tide, creates a buffer that provides protection against coastal erosion.

Such is the ferocity of some winter storms, however, that clumps of kelp are ripped from the seabed and deposited on the beaches as 'tangles'. This cast kelp has proved a valuable natural resource for past generations of islanders who burnt the seaweed to create an ash used in glassmaking.

Today, kelp props up the island's wider ecosystem: the cast seaweed is broken down by invertebrates that, in turn, attract

◀ Cast kelp. Whitemill Bay.

Orkney's Neolithic heart

Although blessed with a rich archaeological heritage encompassing many different periods in history, it is Orkney's Neolithic heritage that is most celebrated. Together, the large chambered tomb at Maes Howe, the ceremonial stone circles at Stenness and Brodgar and the settlement at Skara Brae (all on western Mainland) and several still unexcavated sites paint a picture of Orkney life some 5000 years ago. This collection of sites, known as the Heart of Neolithic Orkney, was inscribed as a World Heritage Site in 1999.

thousands of shoreline birds. It can take a moment for the eyes to adjust, but it soon becomes clear just how many birds are feeding in amongst the tangles. Large numbers of purple sandpiper and turnstone gather on Sanday's east coast, while winter also brings ringed plover, bar-tailed godwit and many other species.

Meanwhile, the living kelp provides food and shelter for a variety of marine life and is an ideal foraging ground for otters, hundreds of common seals and a smaller number of greys. Easily seen around much of Sanday, common seals are present in particularly high numbers on the Holms of Ire during their summer moult, while pups swim and laze with their mothers around

the inlets of Otters Wick.

Other reliable areas for seals, waders and even the occasional otter include the broad tidal bay at Cata Sand and the skerries off Tres Ness and Els Ness.

Although the largest of Orkney's North Isles, Sanday is low lying and perfect for walking or cycling. Don't be tempted to rush, however: with more than 120km of coastline, there is much to explore. The excellent Sanday Trail – available in booklet form at the ferry terminal – covers many key archaeological sites, plus some prime spots for wildlife.

Turnstone feed amongst the cast kelp

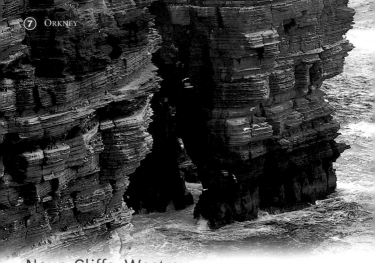

Noup Cliffs, Westray RSPB Reserve

Getting there **Northwest tip of Westray, 6.4km from Pierowall. Ferries and flights from Kirkwall** OS Map **Landranger 5**

The stunningly located Noup Cliffs provide Orkney's most overwhelming seabird experience.

With well over 80,000 individuals, Noup Cliffs hold the largest seabird colony in Orkney by some distance, while Noup Head itself marks the culmination of an 8km-stretch of cliff that runs along Westray's west coast.

Noup Head is a bit special even for seabird cliff aficionados: the sheer density of birds that cling to every available ledge on the sandstone cliffs coupled with the palpable drama of the surroundings is breathtaking. Gazing west, the nearest landfall is somewhere between Greenland and Nova Scotia — an extraordinary distance of fetch that delivers fearsome waves.

Loud, chaotic and with the distinctively pungent aroma found at all large seabird colonies, the cliffs hold around 40,000 guillemots, 20,000 pairs of kittiwake and large numbers of fulmar and razorbill.

Puffins also nest here — although they are better viewed at Castle o'Burrian near Rapness pier — while gannets are the most recent addition to Noup Head's seabird city. Thought to be an overflow from a colony on faraway Sule Stack, gannets first nested here in 2003. Numbers have gradually increased since, with small groups now visible on larger ledges near the lighthouse.

Inland, the pristine maritime heath, a rare habitat largely limited to Orkney and Shetland, harbours high numbers of

◄ Natural arch at the base of Noup Cliffs

breeding waders and, in good years, up to 2000 nesting Arctic terns. Food shortages have, however, resulted in a dramatic reduction in numbers – a problem that has affected the breeding success of many of Orkney's seabirds.

Most visitors reach Noup Cliffs via a track that passes through Noup Farm, although a more energetic and rewarding option is to follow the West Westray Walk – a rugged 8km trek that starts at Kirbest Farm. If time is short, the walk can be joined via a path just north of the wonderful Bis Geos hostel, from where it is a 3km hike up to Noup Head.

Whatever the starting point, hug the cliff edge and be sure to look back at the many geos along the way. North of Bis Geos, seabird numbers begin to increase, while the boulder fields around Monivey are home to pockets of black guillemot. These delightful seabirds, with their bright vermilion feet and gape, often sit in tight groups, their eyes scanning for danger.

As the cliffs rise in stature and the lighthouse comes into view, the noise increases – culminating in a cacophonous din around the head itself. Look out for grey seals hauled out on the skerries far below, while pods of orca are sometimes seen from the headland.

Orkney speciality

Black guillemots calling

The black guillemot (or tystie) is a real Orkney speciality. Unlike their larger cousins that breed in high numbers on the ledges at Noup Cliffs, black guillemots are more thinly scattered, preferring to nest in crevices and on boulder beaches along rocky coastlines. The birds are easily recognised in summer with their white wing patches and oversized red feet. Although wary of bonxies and other predators, black guillemots can be incredibly confiding if approached slowly. It is sometimes even possible to edge close enough to see their stunning gape as the birds call their mournful, high-pitched whistle.

North Hill, Papa Westray RSPB Reserve

Getting there **Ferries and flights from Westray and Kirkwall, Mainland**
OS Map **Landranger 5**

Papa Westray's windswept North Hill holds an all-star cast of wildlife each summer – with close encounters almost guaranteed.

Papa Westray (or just Papay) may be diminutive, but nonetheless exerts quite a pull. Archaeologically rich, with one of Orkney's finest Neolithic sites at Knap of Howar, the island also holds an array of wildlife – with the RSPB reserve at North Hill the centre of activity each summer.

As elsewhere on Orkney, the habitat on North Hill has been shaped by the elements: the exposure and salt air has created a large expanse of maritime heath, a rare habitat characterised by stunted heather and colourful flowering plants. Chief among them is the Scottish primrose, a hardy species that grows in only a handful of places in Orkney and the Scottish mainland.

North Hill has long been used for communal cattle grazing by crofters, with the resulting close-cropped heath and grassland providing a home for up to a thousand pairs of Arctic tern that attempt to breed here in a good season.

And where there are large numbers of terns there are often Arctic skuas – a piratical species that specialises in intimidating the terns into releasing their catch when returning from fishing trips. With as many as 100 pairs of Arctic skuas, plus a handful of great skuas, dramatic aerial chases are common.

However, as on neighbouring Westray, food shortages have hit the terns hard in recent seasons, with overall numbers and breeding productivity dramatically reduced. Terns rely on mass defence to protect eggs and young, which means that the smaller numbers that do attempt to breed are less

Arctic terns are built for long-distance travel

Travelling terns

Arctic terns have a harsh screeching call and are quick to mobilise in defence of nest sites, as anyone unfortunate enough to blunder into a colony knows all too well. Dainty, but tough, the terns breed at high latitudes in the northern hemisphere and winter in Antarctic waters – the longest annual migration of any species. The birds arrive on North Hill in May and attempt to raise up to three chicks in shallow scrapes in the ground. Sandeels are the main prey item, but they will also take small fish such as herring and even flying insects when marine prey is scarce,

able to escape the harrying skuas.

North Hill is reached from the end of the public road that runs north through the island. A hide cum visitor centre – housed in a former coastguard hut – provides information on the reserve, including the 6km coastal trail that visitors are requested to use during the breeding season.

The trail passes the low-lying cliffs at Fowl Craig where close views of guillemot, kittiwake, shag and puffin can all be enjoyed. This is also a prime spot for Scottish primrose with a large colony growing 100m or so inland – best seen when the plant's tiny amethyst flowers open up (in May and again from July to late September).

Further north, past a statue commemorating the UK's last breeding great auk, the boulder beaches hold good numbers of black guillemot, while common and grey seals haul out at Wheelie's Taing to the south. There are also plenty of breeding waders, particularly around the Loch of Hundland.

The RSPB warden, based at nearby Rose Cottage, offers guided walks (April-Aug) and visitors are encouraged to drop in and ask questions.

◀ North Hill in evening light

Geographically (and culturally) closer to Norway than Edinburgh, Shetland is a far-flung collection of more than 100 islands. Distinct from fertile Orkney, Shetland's weathered landscape and wildlife are measured in superlatives with the UK's highest density of otters, dramatic marine life – including killer whales (orcas) – and a bewildering number of birds. Shetland's northerly latitude also brings natural spectacles of its own: the northern lights in winter and the simmer dim (a perpetual twilight) in summer.

This section journeys between two lighthouses at opposite ends of the archipelago: Sumburgh Head in south Mainland and Muckle Flugga off the northernmost tip of Unst – a distance of almost 120km.

In addition to Loch of Spiggie on south Mainland, it includes visits to three of Shetland's finest seabird cliffs – Sumburgh Head, Noss and Hermaness on Unst – plus the magical island of Mousa where a 2000-year-old broch comes alive at night with returning storm petrels.

In the North Isles, Shetland's moorland heart is explored on Yell, while neighbouring Fetlar provides a double treat, with red-throated divers and incredibly confiding red-necked phalaropes.

The section ends with a visit to Fair Isle, situated halfway between Shetland and Orkney and an example of how wildlife tourism can contribute to the viability of an isolated community.

Shetland and Fair Isle

Sumburgh Head RSPB Reserve

Getting there On the southern tip of Mainland, 3.5km south of Sumburgh Airport OS Map Landranger 4

Sumburgh Head offers an introduction to the daily life of a major seabird colony – including some of Shetland's most approachable puffins.

Rising to a height of 100m and pounded by fierce Atlantic swells, the southernmost tip of Mainland Shetland provides ideal breeding conditions for a variety of seabirds. The usual vertical hierarchy is followed with shags nesting at the bottom of the cliffs and fulmar, kittiwake, guillemot and a sprinkling of razorbills further up.

Invariably, however, it is the almost two thousand puffins that inhabit their burrows around the grassy tops that steal the show.

Remaining behind the boundary wall, it is possible to observe them at close quarters, watching as their eyes constantly scan for danger from passing gulls and skuas.

Plenty of seabirds can be spotted even from the main car park, although numbers increase dramatically further up the hill towards the lighthouse. Information boards along the way point to particularly good puffin watching spots. Once at the lighthouse, follow the perimeter path, using the low wall to aid a stealthy approach: the rewards can be great, with some birds almost at touching distance.

In addition to its seabirds, the combination of elevation and the food-rich waters below make Sumburgh Head a top site for whale and dolphin watching (collectively known as cetaceans). Several

A puffin emerges from its burrow

species are often seen from the *Good Shepherd* as it travels past the head to and from Fair Isle.

Harbour porpoise are most commonly spotted, as well as good numbers of Risso's, white-beaked and white sided dolphins. Pods of orcas – the largest dolphins of all – also hunt seals quite close inshore and are seen from Sumburgh Head and in Mousa Sound most summers.

The most common whale in these waters is the minke, although a tendency to surface only briefly makes them tough to spot on anything other than the calmest of days.

The really fortunate may even catch the blow or breaching of a humpback whale.

Sumburgh Head's ease of access makes it popular and it can become swamped by coaches and school parties at the height of summer. Arrive early or late in the day for a more peaceful encounter, and between May and early August for the peak seabird period.

It is possible to stay at Sumburgh Lighthouse – managed by Shetland Amenity Trust and soon to include an RSPB visitor centre. Sumburgh Head can also be accessed using a coastal path from Sumburgh Hotel.

Orca watching

Orcas (killer whales) are one of the most sought-after sights from Sumburgh Head. Highly intelligent and weighing in at up to nine tonnes, orcas are one of the ocean's top predators. Mostly black with distinctive white patches, orcas hunt in well-organised pods feeding on a variety of fish, seals, squid and other cetaceans. They have also been known to scoop up flocks of moulting seabirds bobbing on the surface. Sightings of these powerful animals have increased in recent years with the prime time being April to August. Adult males are often the first to be spotted thanks to their huge dorsal fins (up to 1.8m high).

◀ Sumburgh Head lighthouse and cliffs

Loch of Spiggie RSPB Reserve

Getting there 3.2km north of Sumburgh
Airport, off B9122 at Scousburgh
OS Map Landranger 4

**Used by bathing terns and skuas in
summer, Loch of Spiggie is also one of
Shetland's most important sites for
wintering wildfowl.**

The shallow, freshwater Loch of Spiggie
sprawls over a large parcel of land in the
southwest Mainland, its edges fringed by
fertile farmland. Once a voe (or sea inlet),
the loch is separated from the Bay of
Scousburgh by a bank of dunes and
colourful machair.

Many of Shetland's freshwater lochs are
acidic and relatively lifeless, but not so Loch
of Spiggie: this nutrient-rich body of water
supports a variety of aquatic plants and rare
zooplankton and is one of the most
productive trout fishing lochs in Shetland.

The water is so clear that it is sometimes
possible to see fish swimming in the burn
that trickles down to Spiggie Beach, while
the bridge over the burn offers a chance of
spotting an otter foraging for the plentiful
eels that also use the waterway.

Loch of Spiggie is managed by the RSPB
as part of a nature reserve that includes the
western edge of neighbouring Loch of Brow.
With plenty of good cover and surrounding
marshland, the loch attracts a variety of
breeding waders in summer, plus a handful
of nesting ducks.

As part of its ongoing wetland
management work, the RSPB is trying to
encourage the return of red-necked
phalaropes – a rare wader that once bred
here and which can be seen at close
quarters on Fetlar in the North Isles.

Summer is also a great time to watch
Arctic terns bathing in the shallows, as well

◀ Loch of Spiggie from Bakkasetter

as 'clubs' of non-breeding bonxies. Both species are best seen at the north end where the road passes close to the water's edge.

Tranquil for much of the year, the loch takes on a different shape from mid-September when squadrons of greylag geese and trumpeting whooper swans arrive from Iceland. Several hundred whoopers have gathered here in the past, although numbers fluctuate from year to year. These elegant birds refuel around the loch, with the majority heading further south around mid-November.

The geese, however, remain for the whole winter as do several species of duck with wigeon, teal and goldeneye all present. Between October and early May, the loch also sees a handful of long-tailed duck, an attractive species normally associated with the open sea.

Loch of Spiggie is best viewed from the minor road that travels along much of its length from near the Spiggie Hotel at South Scousburgh. An information board on the boatshed opposite a track to Scousburgh Sands gives an indication of what to expect throughout the year, while the nearby beach is a good spot for a summer swim.

Show ponies

Although their exact roots are unclear, Shetland's famous ponies are one of the most ancient breeds in the UK. Short, shaggy and exceptionally strong, the animals were traditionally used by islanders as a source of muscle, carrying peat for use as fuel and seaweed that was spread as a natural fertiliser on fields. Their small stature and pulling power led to the animals being exported for use in coal mines during the 1800s. Today, they are widely shown at country fairs around the world, but can still be seen wandering around parts of their native islands.

Mousa RSPB Reserve

Getting there **Passenger ferry (mid-April to mid-Sept) from Sandwick (22km south of Lerwick)** OS Map **Landranger 4**

Packed with wildlife during the day, Mousa nonetheless reveals its true magic at night thanks to its remarkable Iron Age broch.

During summer months, the tiny island of Mousa has two sides to its character: one that shows itself during the long daylight hours, and another that emerges briefly in the half-dark, or simmer dim, of a short Shetland night.

During the day, this now uninhabited island is home to a colourful mix of noisy and highly territorial seabirds: the pebble beaches are dotted with nesting Arctic terns, while much of the interior is the domain of Arctic and great skuas. A more easily agitated and aggressive trio is hard to imagine.

The island is served by passenger ferry from Sandwick once or twice each day. On the trip across, scan the water for harbour porpoise, minke whale and even pods of orca that sometimes hunt here between May and September.

Once on Mousa, visitors are asked to follow the trail marker posts on a circular route that runs for roughly 2.5km. The trail takes in the shallow lagoons at the eastern end of the island that are a favourite haul-out site for large numbers

Storm petrel secrets

The UK's smallest seabird, storm petrels are named after St Peter for their habit of appearing to walk on water when feeding. These secretive birds arrive in May and depart in September, spending the rest of the year feeding on plankton far out to sea. They come ashore at night to avoid predators, preferring overcast conditions for extra safety. Each pair takes it in turns to sit at the nest, sometimes waiting for days while the other is at sea. When the chick finally leaves its nest in late-autumn, it begins a 30-year lifetime of annual migration to as far afield as South Africa.

of common seals and smaller groups of greys.

Common seals pup in June and haul out to moult in August and September – at which time numbers around the east and west pools can swell to more than 400 animals. The best views are to be had from behind the wall.

However, in the south of the island, just 1km from the jetty, is Mousa's main draw: a perfectly preserved 2000-year-old broch. The 40-foot high structure is impressive in its own right, but even more so considering what lies within its chambers: more than 6000 storm petrels – or 2 per cent of the world population – nest not only within the structure, but also

outside in the walls and boulder beaches.

Mostly silent during the day, the incubating birds find their voices at dusk to guide their mates back to the nest. When conditions are right, the broch almost vibrates with their purring calls. At first, the returning storm petrels arrive tentatively in ones and twos, until the air becomes alive with birds, each scrabbling to locate their tiny nest entrances in the gloom.

Tom Jamieson, the ferry operator, runs night trips to the island from mid-May to late-July, usually leaving around 11pm and returning well after midnight. Standing outside an ancient broch with hundreds of storm petrels ghosting past is a real Shetland highlight.

◀ Mousa broch in the simmer dim.

Noss Scottish Natural Heritage

Getting there By SNH inflatable boat from Bressay (May-Aug). Reserve closed Monday and Thursday OS Map Landranger 32

A world-class seabird cliff, Noss draws thousands of wildlife enthusiasts and photographers each summer.

Lying off the coast of Bressay, the compact island of Noss slopes gradually up from its western margins to sheer sandstone cliffs that are home to a dozen species of seabird and roughly 100,000 individuals.

Like Hermaness on Unst, Noss's moorland interior is dominated by breeding great skuas (or bonxies) and smaller numbers of Arctic skuas. Both species lay up to two eggs in a shallow scrape on the ground and are fiercely protective of their nest sites. It is not easy, however, for the two to flourish side by side in large numbers and the smaller Arctic skuas have been slowly edged

out by their bulkier relatives.

More than 400 pairs of bonxies now breed on Noss and make their presence felt across the reserve. Although they can catch their own food, bonxies regularly chase other birds to force them to drop food, and also take chicks.

Elsewhere, the sheep that graze freely for much of the year are kept behind a large drystone hill dyke when lambing. This offers protection from the bonxies that are sometimes blamed for killing very young lambs, although ravens and great black-backed gulls are likely just as guilty.

On the cliffs, the heavily weathered sandstone is riddled with ledges and crevices providing ideal nest sites for a huge community of seabirds that includes 45,000 guillemots and 8000 pairs of gannets.

Sadly, and like many major colonies in Scotland, the waters around Noss have suffered from food shortages, resulting in a

◄ Pock marked ledges on the cliffs at Noss

The trouble with sandeels

If seabird colonies are indicators of the overall health of a marine environment then Noss suggests that all is not well. In the past, poor breeding success was blamed by some on the over fishing of sandeels, but that is no longer the case, and the finger is now being pointed at climate change. The suspicion is that a slight rise in sea temperatures is making conditions less suitable for cold-water species such as sandeels. Although widely held, such a belief is hard to prove conclusively given the difficulty of accurately monitoring the state of many marine species.

near total collapse of breeding in some years. A dearth of sandeels – the staple diet of many species that fish close inshore – has forced puffins, kittiwakes and others to seek alternative, and less nutritious, food sources.

Seabirds are long-lived and generally able to ride out a couple of bad seasons, but it is feared that the current situation might be a long-term trend rather than a short-term cycle. More encouragingly, gannets – a relatively recent breeder on Noss – continue to grow in numbers. It is perhaps no coincidence, however, that they can travel great distances to feed and have a more varied diet.

Trails lead up from the landing site and hug the perimeter of the island on a 9km loop, although there are shorter walks that

take in the seabird cliffs. For a different view, join one of the boat trips that operate from Lerwick harbour. One even has an onboard mini submarine that beams back images of life in the trenches and caves beneath the cliffs.

Guillemots nesting near the cliff edge

Yell

Getting there By ferry to Ulsta from Toft, Mainland OS Maps Landranger 1 and 2

Yell's dark moorland shelters a variety of life, while a rich coastline makes it the otter capital of Shetland.

Dominated by bleak and largely uninhabited moorland, Yell is often derided as the ugly duckling of Shetland's North Isles – somewhere to pass through, preferably quickly, on the way to more attractive destinations.

But although stark, Yell's varied moorland holds high numbers of classic Shetland wildlife from red-throated diver on remote lochans to redshank, whimbrel and golden plover amongst the heather. With a little patience and a keen eye, many species can be spotted even from the car.

The moorland between the village of

West Sandwick and the main road is a particularly good area to park up and watch the heather come alive.

Elsewhere, the RSPB manages a remote reserve around the Lochs of Lumbister to the north of Whale Firth. This large area is easily viewed from the main road that travels up the spine of the island, although another option is to drive the narrow track between Dalsetter and Cullivoe. Using a car as a hide is a good way to enjoy vulnerable breeding species without causing disturbance.

Meanwhile, Yell's coastline supports the highest density of otters in Shetland – quite a feat in an island chain where they are hardly in short supply. Yell's secret lies in its habitat, with ample stretches of low-lying peaty shoreline for excavating holts, while supplies of freshwater – essential for

Otter breeding

Male and female otters live separately, only coming together to mate. Although there is no specific breeding season, Scotland's otters do demonstrate a degree of seasonality. In Shetland, most cubs are born in summer, while on Skye, for example, there are two peak periods: early summer and late autumn. The successful rearing of cubs is crucial, given the animals' relatively short reproductive window. Otters only live for around five years and do not breed until aged two. It is all the more reason to drive carefully on Yell and elsewhere: vehicle collisions are a common cause of death for otters.

the animals to clean salt from their fur are rarely far away.

Nimble, opportunistic hunters, otters forage for butterfish and crabs along the shoreline, although they will happily venture inland to take frogs from burns and lochans. Smaller prey items are usually eaten in the water, while larger items are brought ashore – particularly if feeding cubs.

Otters on Yell are active throughout the day, with some of the best views during the short daylight hours of winter. Locals can advise on particular hotspots, although the ferry berths at both Ulsta and Gutcher are usually good places to start.

Elsewhere, try the rocky bay at West

Sandwick, or the north side of Basta Voe around Cunnister and between Kirkabister and the headland at Burraness. A picturesque spot, with an Iron Age broch nearby, the headland can also be reached on foot from North Sandwick.

While exploring sheltered voes, look out, too, for grey and common seals as well as cetaceans that ply the waters off Yell – particularly around Bluemull and Yell Sounds. With the edge of the European Continental Shelf lying close by, deep-water specimens such as humpback whales sometimes veer off track adding to the natural spectacle of this most underrated of islands.

◀ Unst from Hill of Troliva, Yell

Fetlar

Getting there **By ferry from Gutcher, Yell, and Belmont, Unst** OS Map **Landranger 1**

The smallest and most fertile of Shetland's North Isles, Fetlar is known for a wide selection of breeding waders – both rare and familiar.

In old Norse, the name Fetlar means 'island of the fat land' and it is easy to see what attracted early settlers: covered in fine croftland, its vibrant greens stand in marked contrast to the predominant browns of neighbouring Yell.

The RSPB manages a large reserve in the north of the island, although access is discouraged between May and August to minimise disturbance to a community of breeding birds that is impressive even by Shetland's high standards. The Shetland Amenity Trust Ranger does, however, conduct regular guided walks throughout the summer. Ask at the Fetlar Interpretive Centre in Houbie for details.

But the RSPB is not keeping all of Fetlar's natural attractions to itself: most species can be readily seen elsewhere on the island. Nationally important numbers of whimbrel – a smaller relative of the curlew – can be spotted on roadside moorland, while the old airstrip is good for Arctic skuas.

Fetlar's rare serpentine heath was also once home to Britain's only breeding snowy owls: the birds successfully reared young from 1967 until 1975 and were the subject

Flighty phalaropes

Red-necked phalaropes seem to do everything in a hurry. The birds only arrive on Fetlar in late May and are gone again by July or August. The smaller, duller coloured males take care of eggs and young – a rare breeding role reversal – leaving the females free to seek out a second mate with which to lay another batch. Unlike other waders, red-necked phalaropes are equipped with lobed toes that help them swim strongly, even when wintering out at sea.

of close study by celebrated Shetland naturalist Bobby Tulloch. Sadly, none of the birds have been seen for many years.

On the coast, Fetlar's cliffs are alive with breeding seabirds, including colonies of storm petrel and Manx shearwater on Lamb Hoga. Meanwhile, seals loaf in good numbers and otters are relatively widespread. Urie is a good otter-watching spot, while the coastline either side of the old pier at Brough is also a hotspot.

However, the main attraction for many visitors is the Loch of Funzie (pronounced *Finnie*) in the east of the island. Although an unremarkable stretch of water, the loch and adjacent mire is home to 90 per cent of the UK's breeding population of red-necked phalaropes.

These rare, but incredibly tame, waders can be seen at very close quarters – a blur of perpetual motion as they flit, feed and squabble at the water's edge. Much work has gone into improving the mire habitat adjacent to the loch for these tiny birds, with considerable success. While phalarope numbers have dropped elsewhere in the UK, Fetlar now holds 20 to 30 pairs. An RSPB hide overlooks the breeding mire.

An early morning visit can also be rewarded with close roadside views of red-throated diver – a demonstrative and charismatic summer visitor to remote Shetland lochs. With luck, it is possible to watch the birds exhibit a full range of complex behaviour before they head out to feed at sea.

◀ Sunset from the Ness of Brough

Hermaness, Unst Scottish Natural Heritage

Getting there **Northern tip of Unst,
follow B9086 signposted to Burrafirth**
OS Map Landranger 1

**Part moorland rite of passage, part
clifftop spectacular, Hermaness offers
close encounters with Shetland's most
charismatic species.**

It would feel anti-climactic if the most
northerly point in Britain proved to be a
lifeless lump of rock that just fell away into
the sea. Fortunately, Hermaness rises to its
sense of place with one of Shetland's most
dramatic wildlife spectacles.

Dominated by peaty moorland and
studded with lochans, Hermaness is home
to the world's third largest colony of great
skuas (bonxies). Once nearly lost to hunters
and egg collectors, the population of these
piratical birds now tops 650 pairs.

The bonxies can thank Laurence
Edmondston for their recovery: the former

landowner instructed employees to protect
the birds back in the 1830s. A keen
naturalist, Edmondston was also the first to
recognise the importance of the alpine plants
found on the rare fell field habitat at nearby
Keen of Hamar.

An aggressive species, bonxies can make
life difficult for their neighbours: much of their
food is robbed from other seabirds, while they
also predate each other's nests and those of
their more graceful cousin, the Arctic skua.

Walkers also need to pay attention: while a
close approach to these supremely self-
assured birds is possible, dive-bombing is not
uncommon. Bonxies rarely connect, but the
sight and sound of such a large bird flashing
past is not soon forgotten.

The path that winds up Hermaness Hill
crosses prime bonxie territory before ending
in dramatic fashion at sea cliffs that reach a
height of 170m in places. The cliffs and
outlying stacks hold a diverse colony of more

◀ The huge gannetry at Neap

than 100,000 seabirds, including 50,000 puffins and a huge gannetry.

Once at the cliff edge, it is worth detouring south to savour the sight and smell of the main gannetry in the bowl like face beyond Neap. There are puffins along the way, plus an opportunity to view gannets nesting close to the cliff edge.

Return north along the same path, skirting the cliff edge as the track heads past the principal puffin viewing area – a rewarding place to be in late afternoon when many birds return from feeding at sea.

The track continues to give views out to Muckle Flugga lighthouse before heading inland to the brow of Hermaness Hill. Surveying the surrounding moorland, it is difficult to imagine other birds prospering amidst so many bonxies, but dunlin, snipe and golden plover all breed here in good numbers. The lochans also hold red-throated divers, whose eerie calls can be heard drifting over the boggy expanse.

A round trip of Hermaness is almost 7km, although SNH prefers walkers to retrace their steps rather than use the now heavily eroded path back through the middle of the reserve.

Moorland bruiser

The name bonxie is derived from the Norse 'bunksie', meaning thick set. Although expert scavengers, bonxies also harass other seabirds into dropping their catch and, increasingly, predate puffins and kittiwakes. Even birds as large as gannets are sometimes forced into the water and drowned. Interestingly, their presence does not seem to affect red-throated divers and could even be beneficial. The divers on Hermaness and elsewhere with large densities of bonxies have consistently higher breeding success than average for Shetland.

Fair Isle National Trust for Scotland

Getting there Ferry from Grutness, Mainland. Flights from Lerwick OS Map Landranger 4

A visit to Fair Isle offers adventure, wildlife and a valuable insight into one of the UK's most successful remote communities.

In bird-watching circles, the name Fair Isle is synonymous with the rarities that are regularly ecorded, particularly during spring and autumn migrations. Lying halfway between Shetland and Orkney on the intersection of many northern European flight paths, the island is a welcome landfall for exhausted birds or those just blown off course.

But while a magnet for serious birders, the island also offers an opportunity for all visitors to be part of a pioneering wildlife tourism project – the Fair Isle Bird Observatory. Although most of the 70 or so islanders live on crofts in the south of the island, it is the Observatory that is the hub of Fair Isle life.

And just getting here is an adventure. Most visitors arrive by the *Good Shepherd*, a supply boat cum ferry that operates three times per week during the summer and lifeline services in the winter. The trip is lumpy at best, but on clear days offers a good chance of spotting whales and dolphins.

As well as being a migration hotspot, Fair Isle also holds more than 100,000 pairs (and 18 species) of breeding seabirds – including huge numbers of very approachable puffins. It is one of five sites used by the Joint Nature Conservation

Recording rarities – an Arctic warbler from Siberia

Committee to monitor the health of British seabird populations.

Sadly, the Fair Isle experience in recent seasons mirrors that of other major seabird stations in Shetland, with widespread breeding failures. A lack of food is to blame (particularly sandeels) resulting in fewer breeding attempts and poor fledging success.

Observatory staff also undertake a daily migrant census of the island and guests are encouraged to participate. This includes joining early morning rounds to record and ring species caught in the various traps set around the Observatory. Other hands-on opportunities include the ringing of puffins and storm petrels during summer months.

In mid-July, guests can also assist in the hair-raising task of searching the moorland for Arctic skua and bonxie chicks. Fair Isle is one of the few places in Shetland where Arctic skuas appear to outnumber their larger cousins, although this is more to do with a particularly aggressive defence of nest sites than actual weight of numbers.

For Observatory staff, any disappointments in seabird performance are compensated for in the autumn. During September and October, the Observatory is invariably fully booked with birders eager to see their first Pechora pipit or Pallas's grasshopper warbler. The island is scoured from head to toe, with many of the rare migrants found around the croftland. Fortunately, islanders are very tolerant of visiting birdwatchers.

Observatory beginnings

Ornithologist George Waterston first conceived a blueprint for formal scientific research on Fair Isle when he visited the island in 1935. He fine-tuned his vision while serving in a prisoner-of-war camp during the Second World War. Once released, Waterston purchased the island from the Sumburgh Estate and opened the Bird Observatory in 1948. The island was subsequently taken over by the National Trust for Scotland, although the Observatory remained in the hands of a separate trust. Today, it accommodates up to 30 guests between April and October.

◄ Sheep Rock at sunet

Index

Hynish Bay on Tiree